PROFILING EXCELLENCE IN AMERICA'S SCHOOLS

John E. Roueche and
George A. Baker, III

with Patricia L. Mullin and
Nancy Hess Omaha Boy

Published by the
American Association
of School Administrators

1801 North Moore Street,
Arlington, Virginia
22209-9988

Other AASA publications promoting excellence in education include:

- Skills for Successful School Leaders
- Evaluating Educational Programs
- Evaluating Educational Personnel
- Effective Instructional Management
- The Role of the Principal in Effective Schools
- Time on Task (book and video)
- Building Morale. . . Motivating Staff
- Improving Math & Science Education
- High Tech for Schools
- Raising Standards in Schools
- Teaching Writing
- Excellence in Our Schools. . . Making It Happen
- The Excellence Report. . . Using It To Improve Your Schools

These publications and more are available from the American Association of School Administrators, 1801 North Moore Street, Arlington, Virginia 22209-9988. Price lists available. Discounts on multiple copy orders. AASA members receive the monthly magazine of the profession, *The School Administrator,* and many other member services.

Stock #021-00157
Library of Congress Card Catalogue #86-70022
ISBN #0-87652-106-5
Copyright 1986 The American Association of School Administrators, Arlington, Virginia. The points of view expressed in this book are those of the authors and do not necessarily reflect the official position or policies of AASA.

Graphics: Domus Design Studios, Inc.

This book is dedicated to Valleau Wilkie, Jr., Executive Vice President of the Sid W. Richardson Foundation, Fort Worth, Texas; to the Board of the Sid W. Richardson Foundation; and to those teachers, principals, and superintendents who strive to keep American education excellent.

CONTENTS

FOREWORD

The American people have great expectations for their schools.
That's healthy. However, those expectations aren't always
clearly defined. People simply want the schools to be effective, and
they want students to learn.

It is up to us, then, to define excellence and to point out examples of what works. Peters and Waterman did just that in profiling excellence in American business. *Profiling Excellence in
America's Schools* takes a similar approach, but its focus is teaching
and administration in our nation's schools.

While this important book is based on a study of secondary
schools, its findings and suggestions will be of interest to everyone
concerned about learning. The American Association of School
Administrators (AASA) found the work of authors John E. Roueche
and George A. Baker, III of The University of Texas at Austin
challenging, sure to spark discussions that would lead to better
education for all students.

We are grateful to the Sid W. Richardson Foundation for providing funds that made it possible for AASA to produce this publication. We urge every educational leader to consider the results of this
study, including the dozens of suggestions, in planning for school
improvement.

Profiling Excellence in America's Schools is one of a series of
examples of AASA's commitment to instructional excellence and
high quality education for our society.

RICHARD D. MILLER, PH.D.
EXECUTIVE DIRECTOR
AMERICAN ASSOCIATION OF SCHOOL ADMINISTRATORS (AASA)

PREFACE

W e are certain that our readers' files are bulging with reports, newsclips, copies of speeches, minutes of boards of education and community group meetings, and summaries of television documentaries that are calling for drastic reforms to make America's schools more effective

Our own files are bulging too. They tell about the more than 40 states that have initiated reforms raising standards for student achievement, setting stiffer requirements for teacher certification and performance, acknowledging the need for better staff development programs, calling for a de-emphasis on athletics, and recognizing the importance of effective administrative leadership to make it all happen.

Those of us who work in American colleges and universities have studied, indirectly, the results of education in American public schools. Although our nation's schools graduate more students and send more on to higher education than in any other nation, many of the first-year students in our open-access institutions have needed remedial work in one or more academic skills. Even our most selective institutions, for example, Harvard, Stanford, UCLA, and Duke, have had to enroll significant numbers of our talented, gifted students in remedial work (Roueche, Baker, and Roueche, 1984).

And who or what must respond to these concerns, formally and informally expressed? Although many American public schools have been awash in a sea of indecision leading to mediocrity for the past decade or longer, a select few have remained firmly on course, well-focused on the dual goals of teaching excellence and student achievement. To recognize some of these schools, the Department of Education under the leadership of then Secretary of Education T.H. Bell, set up a national program, the Secondary School Recognition Program (SSRP), to identify, recognize, and reward some of the nation's most outstanding secondary schools.

This program, initiated in 1982, continues to call attention annually to a national group of schools that are unusually effective in educating their students. In selecting the schools, the SSRP also seeks to identify those that have been successful in overcoming obstacles and problems and that are continuing to work hard toward improvement. As well, it recognizes schools that implement successful programs, practices, and policies that research and experience identify as contributors to positive student outcomes. A major goal of the program is to identify and recognize examples of good practice in the hope of stimulating other schools to engage in improvement efforts.

In selecting these schools, the SSRP uses two groups of criteria for success. The first group is a collection of 14 school characteristics associated with effectiveness, and the second identifies five areas of student outcomes.

The 14 school characteristics are:

1. Clear academic and behavioral goals
2. Order and discipline
3. High expectations for students
4. Teacher efficacy
5. Rewards and incentives for teachers and students
6. Positive school environment
7. Administrative leadership
8. Community support
9. Extent of concentration on academic learning time
10. Frequent and monitored homework
11. Regular and frequent monitoring of student progress
12. Well-coordinated curriculum
13. Variety of teaching strategies
14. Opportunities for student responsibility.

The five areas of outcomes are:

1. Percentage of students who go on to attend some form of postsecondary education or training and the number who received scholarships
2. Number of students who were successful in academically-oriented competitions, such as science fairs and essay contests
3. Student dropout rates
4. Student performance on other standardized measures of achievement (for example, SAT's, PSAT's, ACT's).

The selection process begins in each state with the Chief State School Officer's submitting nominations of secondary schools to two panels of nonfederal, educational experts in Washington, D.C. The two 15-member panels—one for high schools and the other for middle/junior high schools—in turn review the applications completed by each nominated school, make onsite visits to validate and enrich information, and then select the most effective schools. Our study of educational excellence examined recipient schools of the 1983 Excellent School Awards issued by the Department of Education and President Reagan.

During the spring of 1984, we visited with Valleau Wilkie, executive vice-president of the Sid W. Richardson Foundation, Fort Worth, Texas, regarding our interest in a study of teaching excellence in the American secondary schools selected by the Department of Education's Secondary School Recognition Program. The Richardson Foundation has a solid history of interest in and support of programs to improve the quality of American schools. Wilkie invited us to submit a proposal to the Foundation for support of our study. The Richardson grant in April 1984 launched our investigation of America's best schools and teachers.

While our conceptual base and research design are discussed in detail later, we feel it is important to say that we strongly believe excellence is found by searching for it. We were not interested in another study of the status quo of teaching and learning in American schools. Rather, we wanted to study in depth the best teachers and principals in, and the climate of, some of the nation's exceptional secondary schools.

Chapter 1 summarizes problems and solutions proposed in the numerous studies resulting from the current reform movement in American education. This chapter then introduces the Model of Excellent Schools resulting from the Roueche-Baker study and presents an overview of the findings.

Chapter 2 presents results of the study related to the type of school climate found in effective secondary schools. In this chapter, five climate factors depicting a favorable learning environment are defined and described.

Chapter 3 elaborates on the seven attributes indicative of effective leadership found in excellent secondary schools. This chapter presents our findings, accompanied by anecdotal quotations from participating principals, regarding the characteristics found among principals who create and guide exceptional schools. The seven attributes are paralleled with the eight Peters and Waterman principles of sound leadership.

Chapter 4 presents the findings concerning the teaching that takes place in outstanding schools. Twelve teacher themes are defined and illustrated with numerous anecdotal examples submitted by participating teachers that reflect the commitment and sentiments of those who are truly dedicated to excellent teaching and to the students they teach.

Chapter 5 presents a summary of the study. It gives a brief recount of the major components of our investigation into teaching excellence in secondary schools. Implications of our conclusions for school boards, administrators, and teachers are also discussed.

CHAPTER 1
SCHOOLING IN AMERICA

T he numerous educational reform reports published in the early 1980s communicated deep concern for the state of American secondary schools. Paul Copperman, in *A Nation at Risk*, the National Commission on Excellence in Education report, noted:

> Each generation of Americans has outstripped its parents in education, in literacy, and in economic attainment. For the first time in the history of our country, the educational skills of one generation will not surpass, will not equal, will not even approach, those of their parents (p.11).

This concern echoed conclusions reached in John Naisbitt's *Megatrends*: "It is more and more apparent that young high school—even college—graduates cannot write English or even do acceptable arithmetic. For the first time in American history, the generation moving to adulthood is less skilled than its parents" (p.9).

The "average achievement of high school students is now lower than 26 years ago when Sputnik was launched," say the writers of *A Nation at Risk:* "The College Board's Scholastic Aptitude Tests (SAT) demonstrate a virtually unbroken decline from 1963 to 1980" (p.8). According to *High School: A Report of the Carnegie Foundation for the Advancement of Teaching*, results of a 12-nation study of scores in seven subjects showed that test scores of U.S. students were in the lowest third in reading, at the lowest in math, and tied with the lowest in civics (Boyer, 1983).

We set out to answer two questions: (1) why this decline in scholarship and (2) what could be done about it. As a first step, we examined the recent reform studies conducted by the various national commissions and discovered that educational experts shared four conclusions—conclusions as striking in their similarities as they are disconcerting in their import.

The Four Conclusions

1. Our Schools Ask Too Little Time of Students.
"Among the world's industrialized nations, the United States

appears to expect the least of its youth in terms of academic achievement," the Education Commission of the States says in its *Action for Excellence* report. Time—or the lack of time—is a major cause. Students in the United States spend a short time in school compared to those in other industrialized nations. In England and other developed countries, a typical school day is eight hours and a school year is 220 days. In contrast, the usual school day in the United States is six hours and the school year is 180 days. In addition, as *A Nation at Risk* points out, less class time is spent on the "solids"; in many other industrialized countries students spend about three times more hours on mathematics, biology, chemistry, physics, geography, and so on than even the most science-oriented U.S. students (pp. 20-21).

The various reports criticized insufficient time spent on language arts, particularly writing skills. Time spent on study after school fared no better. "The amount of homework for high school seniors has decreased (two-thirds report less than one hour a night), and grades have been rising as average student achievement has been declining," observe the writers of *A Nation at Risk* (p. 20).

2. We Ask Too Little Mental Effort of Students.

M.J. Adler, in *The Paiedeia Problems and Possibilities,* claimed:

> Most of the teaching which occurs in our classrooms results in stuffing of the memory, not growth of the mind....When a teacher tries to play the primary role of imparting knowledge, passively received and without its being understood, only the student's memory is affected, not his mind....Most of the remembered information is subsequently forgotten; and the student's mind at the end of the process is no better off than it was at the beginning (pp. 23-24).

John I. Goodlad called this kind of teaching "teacher talk" in his "Study of Schooling: Some Findings and Hypotheses" published in the April 1983 *Phi Delta Kappan.* In the classrooms of 38 schools of varying characteristics, he estimated that once teacher talk and housekeeping chores are completed, only

> 12 percent of available class time was spent on a combination of observing demonstrations...discussions... simulation and roleplaying, reading, and activity involving the use of audiovisual equipment....This picture... becomes even more monotonous when classes in academic subjects are separated from data related to the arts, physical education, and vocational education....The feedback-with-guidance associated with helping students

to understand and correct their mistakes was almost nonexistent (p. 467).

Others agreed that Goodlad's characterization best describes the vast majority of American secondary schools. Theodore R. Sizer illustrated an identical situation, in *Horace's Compromise: The Dilemma of the American High School Today,* when he described an archetypal class in which one-third of the time was spent on noninstructional activities. Two-thirds of instructional time was spent mostly on orderly teacher talk, in other words, lecturing. The teacher's room "was quiet, and his students like him....He had the esteem of [his principal]....[The teacher] and his class had [rapport] all right, agreement that reduced the efforts of both students and teacher to an irreducible and pathetic minimum" (p. 156).

Others have reported this kind of "agreement." Ernest L. Boyer and members of the commission funded by the Carnegie Foundation for the Advancement of Teaching, likewise, reported that "at Ridgefield (pseudonym) and elsewhere, there is a kind of unwritten, unspoken contract between the teachers and the students: Keep off my back and I'll keep off yours" (p. 16).

3. We Allow—Even Encourage—Students to Take Too Many Inconsequential Courses.

Boyer, in *High School,* advocated the adoption of a core of common learning. According to this commission, many students had rejected academic and some vocational courses that would provide much of this common core and were spending a lot of their time in courses that might be described as personal service and social development. Boyer called for greater emphasis on the study of consequential ideas, experiences, and traditions common to all members of society. Boyer pointed out that students were divided into programs for those who "think" and those who "work," when a blend of both is what is needed, especially since today's graduates will face the need to acquire new skills throughout life. The curriculum as it was did not provide a foundation for lifelong learning.

What do Americans want their high schools to accomplish? "Quite simply," says Boyer, "we want it all" (p. 57). Our curriculum certainly tries. However, offering many attractive-sounding, easy courses diminished the importance of academic courses by saying officially that minimal expectations were enough. What conclusions could we expect students to draw?

Bringing continuity to the presently fragmented curriculum is essential, Boyer argued. He believes that greater emphasis on more transcendent issues will help move a group of relatively unrelated courses toward coherence. More specifically, Boyer and the commission called for a strengthening of traditional courses in literature, history, mathematics, and science, as well as greater emphasis on foreign language, the arts, civics, non-Western studies, technology, the meaning of work, and the importance of health.

4. We Tolerate—Even Encourage—Ineffective Teaching.

A basic assumption underlying the reports' criticisms of the state of teaching in our schools was that the adverse conditions being reported had been around for a long time; hence, they must not have bothered us too much. Otherwise, we would have done something about them. "Much teaching in high schools is abysmal," asserted Sizer,

> [W]hile some of this clearly is due to teachers' incompetence, insensitivity, and carelessness, some also flows from the conditions of work…the demeaning attitudes, *and the public policies which flow from them* (author's emphasis), with which the public treats the profession. America and its teachers are in a cul-de-sac of attitudes and practice (p. 184).

In *A Nation at Risk,* the language was more blunt: "The professional working life of teachers is unacceptable" (p. 22). What were the "unacceptable" working conditions? First, salaries in comparison to other professions were (and still are in many instances) too low. *A Nation at Risk* placed the "average salary after twelve years of teaching" at $14,000 per year (p. 22).

Second, individual teachers had little influence in important educational decisions and were rarely trusted with the selection of the texts and rarely consulted, much less given significant authority, over the rules and regulations governing the life of their school (Sizer, 1984).

Third, the preponderance of lecturing and lack of time-on-task was an accepted part of all schools, and both teachers and their publics were generally satisfied with the situation. Furthermore, satisfaction with the current curriculum and its primary teaching method generally existed among parents and teachers. Small wonder that outstanding persons are not entering teaching. "Half the newly employed math, science, and English teachers are not qualified to teach in those subjects," according to the authors of *A Nation at Risk* (p. 23). "Too many teachers are being drawn from the bottom quarter of graduating high school and college students," that study asserts (p. 23). Other reports pointed out that SAT scores for students preparing to be teachers were 80 points below the national *average*. This fact was disturbing, but it is probably what we should expect, given the working conditions they can expect to find as teachers.

Proposed Solutions

Many of the reports did much more than decry the state of the nation's schooling. They included recommendations for improvement, as well as suggestions for methods that might work. Rarely, however, did they recommend solutions to the usual mega-problems like adequate financing and genuine integration. Instead, their suggestions most often focused on overlooked problems such as *educational leadership, expectations of students, expectations of teachers, what students are unconsciously taught (and are not taught),* and *what students are taught by the methods used (or not used) to teach them.*

1. What Can Be Done? We Ask Too Little of Students.

Ask more! At a minimum, says *A Nation at Risk,*

> [T]he time available for learning should be expanded through better classroom management and organization of the school day....Additional time should be found to meet the needs of slow learners, the gifted, and others who need more instructional diversity than can be accommodated during a conventional school day or year (p. 29).

As for homework, reports call for more to be assigned. They warn, however, that homework must not be busywork. Most reports point out that increasing the amount of near-worthless homework is useless, obviously, and most likely counterproductive. Further, homework "must be carefully examined and corrected by the teacher. Without teacher evaluation, it comes to nothing. Moreover, parental support of homework is needed to see that it is done effectively" (Adler, 1982, p. 54).

2. What Can Be Done? We Ask Too Little Mental Effort of Students.

One answer to the question requires a prior agreement: that teaching methods vary. The "lecture method," the overuse of which is criticized by various reports, is but one. Adler's *Paideia Problems* presents a reasonable delineation of teaching methods:

The three modes of teaching (which correlate with the three modes of learning—knowledge, skills, and understanding) are: (1) the didactic, which is teaching by telling or lecturing, aided by textbooks, manuals, recitations, demonstrations, quizzes, and examinations; (2) coaching which is teaching by supervising performances to attain skills (for every skill is acquired by habit formation), and good habits, which skills are, result from repeated acts under the guidance of a seasoned performer who is a coach; (3) Socratic or "maieutic" teaching, which is teaching by asking or questioning (not telling or lecturing, and certainly not coaching). Socratic teaching is most effectively done in seminars, in which students engage in free discussion that is kept on track by a leader, the materials discussed being either books (books that are not textbooks) or productions of quality in other fields of art and thought (pp. 16-17).

Virtually all reports that discuss teaching methods strongly emphasize that "coaching" and "Socratic teaching" are rarely found in our schools. Most teaching time (that excludes class time spent on noninstructional affairs) is "'teachertalk' time—memory stuffing." This must change if we decide to require more mental effort of our students.

In order for more "coaching" and "Socratic" teaching to occur, four powerful anchors need to be pulled from the mud. First, the overemphasis on facts needs to be placed in a more appropriate perspective. Where competency tests (which presumably measure the things schools believe to be most important) exist, they must measure more than students' basic knowledge. We must teach in ways that help students "differentiate and see the relationships between facts and the more important concepts which help us to understand, (and) to view subjects and subject matter as merely turf on which to experience the struggles and satisfactions of personal development" (Goodlad, 1984, p. 552). That is not an easy task. As Goodlad points out in *A Place Called School*, "[a]t all levels of schooling...curricular sameness characterize[s] the topical organization, factual organization, textbook content, and the things tested. The emphasis is on recall, not problem solving or inquiry" (p. 552).

Second, the format of the school day needs to change to accommodate "coaching" and "Socratic teaching" methods. A school day of rigid time periods during which a teacher meets 120-150 students encourages lecturing. Adler suggests a weekly format that provides 60 percent of the time for "the acquisition of subject matter knowledge," 30 percent for "coaching in the development of intellectual skills," and 10 percent for "seminar discussion" (1983, pp. 16-17).

Changing to this format need not involve major new technologies, custom-built furniture, or renovations to buildings.

Third, since teachers tend to teach the same way they were taught, and since they were taught predominately by the lecture method, a vicious circle of teaching technique exists; the cycle must be broken. Doing so need not be arduous or mysterious. In methods courses or inservice workshops, prospective and current teachers can be taught the skills of "coaching" and "Socratic teaching." They *are* skills; they can be learned; they can be polished by practice. And, yes, some teachers will be more skillful than others, just as some are better at lecturing than others.

Fourth, we need to admit to ourselves that lecturing is *easy*. It is far less demanding for both students and teacher, requiring less intellectual and physical engagement than other methods.

Students' mental effort would also be increased, some reports suggest, if periodic tests of general achievement and specific skills were used to measure their progress and if mastery, not age, determined promotion from grade to grade.

In general, the reports assert that "more of the same" is insufficient. The nature of classroom teaching—as well as the kinds of courses taught, in particular—needs to change. Without that change, the problems, as identified by the reports, will be intensified.

3. What Can Be Done? We Allow—Even Encourage— Students to Take Too Many Inconsequential Courses.

In response to our "smorgasbord curriculum," several reports urgently called for increased numbers of courses in "solids," particularly in math, science, and English, and many communities and legislatures responded. *A Nation at Risk* recommends that high school students take (a) four years of English, (b) three years of mathematics, (c) three years of social studies, and (d) one-half year of computer science. For the college bound, two years of foreign language are strongly recommended, in addition to any foreign language taken prior to entering high school (p. 24). The recommendations of other reports were similar. Some wisely included major goals for the courses.

Adding is the easy part. Subtracting is the tougher. Significantly, except for broad generalizations and by implication, no report suggested *what*, from the smorgasbord curriculum, to delete. There are three probable reasons for this omission, two obvious and one subtle: (1) there are simply too many electives, even categories of electives, from which to compile a national hit list; (2) many electives were born of the labors of local and state pressure groups or influential teachers who wanted "pet" courses; and (3) the public was generally satisfied with the curriculum. As Goodlad reports, curriculum, which tends to be the same in all schools, was not rated as a salient concern in schools characterized as "most satisfying" or in those characterized as "least satisfying."

What can be done about students taking too many inconsequential courses? One answer is to require more consequential courses and allow fewer inconsequential ones. But no one should underestimate the difficulty at the local level of listing which courses fit into which category.

4. What Can Be Done? We Tolerate—Even Encourage—Inadequate Teaching.

To have adequate teaching in our classrooms, we must have good teachers. To this end, most reports asked for better working conditions: higher pay, greater respect, more voice in decision making, differentiated staffing, new reward systems, and career ladders. Esteem for teaching as a profession must also be restored.

Several reports pleaded for more autonomy for schools and for individual teachers. When teachers do not have, or feel they do not have, an important voice in making decisions about, for instance, curriculum and instructional materials, they do not feel professionally involved or trusted.

Inadequate teaching cannot be tolerated. "Salary, promotion, tenure, and retention decisions should be tied to an evaluation system," bluntly stated *A Nation at Risk*, "...so that superior teachers can be rewarded, average ones encouraged, and poor ones either improved or terminated" (p. 30).

Central to the process of improving and maintaining quality instruction is the principal. Goodlad, for instance, in *A Place Called School*, called selecting (or developing) principals who can lead and manage a superintendent's first order of business (p. 227).

Though they do not attempt to gloss over financial problems nor to avoid the probability that large infusions of money will probably be necessary to help make our schooling better, the various reports do find excellence. It's rare. Good schools were termed "oases," good teachers "heroic." The reports found excellence predictably in some private, selective schools, but they also found it occasionally in inner city schools with predominately black and Hispanic enrollments. The principal of one such inner city school provided an example of excellent, creative leadership. When confronted with "downtown's" indifference to his requests for badly needed paint for the halls and classrooms of his school and the union's hostility toward do-it-youselfers, he covered the school's walls with murals—student art. Confronted by lack of funds and support, he did not give up but discovered a way to solve the problem despite the obstacles.

Finding such glimmerings of excellence amid the "gloom and doom" gave many of the nation's reports a sense of optimism. *A Nation at Risk* even titled one of its final sections, "America Can Do It." This section begins: "Despite the obstacles and difficulties that inhibit the pursuit of superior intellectual achievement, we are confident, with history as our guide, that we can meet our goal" (p. 33).

Similarly, we who have undertaken this study also believe that *excellence is found by searching for it.* That is, excellence is found not by studying the status quo, but by studying successful schools, successful administrators, successful teachers, and in a causal fashion, successful learners.

Kappa Delta Pi's study, *One Hundred Good Schools,* makes the point in a different way. The authors concluded that excellence is: (1) unrelated to level of education, to public or private control; (2) independent of the age of the students or their learning achievements; (3) independent of wealth or geographical location; and (4) not necessarily determined by socioeconomic status. The study concluded that motivated administrators, teachers, and learners can take the status quo and change mediocrity into quality and excellence.

We wondered how such success was achieved and decided to investigate the relationship between the actions of successful principals and teachers and the achievements of successful students.

Excellence, whether it is defined as a benchmark, that is "to be superior to," or as a point on a continuum, meaning "to surpass in achievement," is a complex concept. Our national concept of excellence is one of striving and accomplishing, of discipline and sacrifice, and of perpetual upward mobility.

Many of the national studies of American schools urged a return to the standards of the past. While that suggestion may be comforting, we need to acknowledge the new era in which we are now living. New demands exert new pressures on all, especially on the educational system. Because education is a social vehicle and because schools comprise a key component of American society, it is critical to understand that the expectations of our society are indeed reflected in the quality of education. Thus, educational reformists cannot afford, as some critics would have it, merely to

return to the old modes or standards as a sole means of improvement. Granted, much can be gained from historical perspective, yet
responsiveness to a changing world is even more critical. Hence,
the revitalization of education must result in an appropriate vehicle
that conveys values and skills necessary for developing people into
contributing members of society who can act and function with
confidence in a changing world full of uncertainty and challenge.

The 1985 Roueche-Baker Study

Many contemporary social science researchers are finding that an
effective way to discover how success is achieved is to study the
behaviors and actions of those who excel at what they do. We use
this approach in our study. Through action research techniques
advocated by David McClelland and his associates, we have arrived
at Figure 1, our "Integrated Model of Excellent Schools." For the
school climate aspects we drew heavily from the work of the Secondary School Recognition Program of the Department of Education.
Our framework of effective principal characteristics was based on
the best seller, *In Search of Excellence,* by Thomas J. Peters and
Robert H. Waterman, Jr. The Teaching Excellence Themes were
organized under the categories developed by the Selection Research
Inc. of Lincoln, Nebraska. The student outcomes aspect of the
model flow from general findings of path-goal leadership theory.
For further description of our research protocols, see Appendix D.

As indicated in the reports' recommendations, much revitalization of education can be achieved through improved selection and
development of people—of those who teach and of those who run
schools. Our findings support the view that organizational climate,
administrative leadership, and teaching excellence are the key
variables in identifying, documenting, or building excellent schools.
We believe that the attributes of climate and the qualities of people
identified in our study can provide superintendents, school boards,
and principals with guidelines for hiring, evaluating, and developing the people who work in their schools.

This chapter began with a summary of four conclusions that
appeared as common threads running through the reform reports of
education in America. First, our schools ask too little time of
students. Second, we ask too little mental effort of students. Third,
we allow students to take too many inconsequential courses. Finally,
we tolerate ineffective teaching.

The reports proposed solutions to these problems, such as asking more time of students, requiring more mental effort from them,

FIGURE 1.
**Roueche-Baker Integrated Model
of Excellent Schools.**

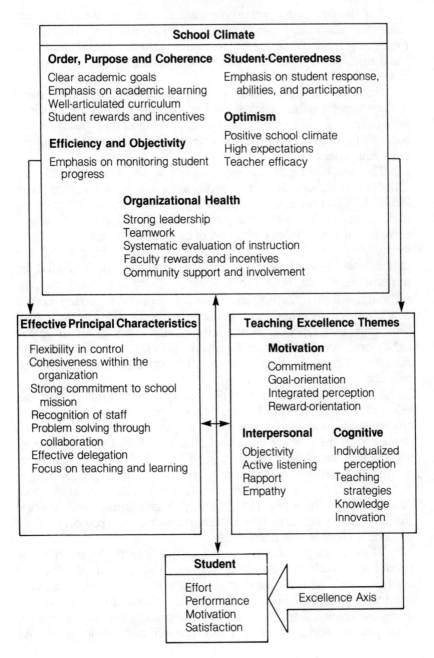

revising curriculum to eliminate inconsequential courses, and improving teaching through selection, evaluation, development, and reward.

For the most part, we wholeheartedly support these proposed solutions. Essentially much of what needs changing involves no major new technologies, fancy furniture, or architectural changes to buildings. On the contrary, what needs changing can be corrected at very little expense.

However, the proposed changes require strong commitment and agreement within each school and school district on the direction change should take. This type of fundamental change is far more difficult to accomplish than ripping out walls and purchasing new equipment.

The results of our study presented in this book should help schools and school districts choose a means by which they can establish direction toward improving the education delivered by their systems. By identifying characteristics of effective school climates, of strong leadership, and of exceptional teaching, we have formulated models of school, leadership, and teaching excellence that can guide decisions for improving education. It should be remembered that these are models and are not exact recipes. Although uniquely expressed by each individual, recurring themes or attributes have emerged from the works and actions of exceptional principals and teachers when empirically investigated using the Behavioral Event Interview Technique (BEIT) of analysis (Klemp et al., 1977). Certainly, these models offer portraits of educational excellence.

A major finding of our study clearly indicates that the schools selected as outstanding are not necessarily unusual nor is there anything atypical about the student populations they serve. As described in the chapter on school climate, the students and settings represent a cross section of our society. The schools are rural, urban, and suburban; are small, medium and large; have high, medium, and low minority representation; and are well-off to poor financially. Yet, the schools in our study do great things with average students and transform typical environments into prototypical institutions. How is this possible?

Attention to people makes the difference. People are the key variable in building excellent schools. The principals and the teachers, along with the support staff, collaborate in achieving quality education through dynamic leadership, effective instruction, and student activities. Together, teachers and principals create a positive atmosphere conducive to student growth and achievement. As

Edison said:"Genius is 1 percent inspiration and 99 percent perspiration." Similarly, Michelangelo stated:"If people knew how hard I worked to get my mastery, it wouldn't seem so wonderful after all." Therefore, focusing on people in a fashion that results in hard work, team effort, and a strong commitment to shared values and goals is the trademark of exceptional schools.

Focus on People

As many have recommended, attention to structure is necessary for the improvement of education. Rightly speaking, heavier emphasis on the "solid" subjects and increased time on task that results in real learning is a necessary part of improving education. Although a tightening of rules and regulations and raising of standards are important, it must be remembered that they represent only one dimension of the changes that must occur. Structure imposed without a positive attitude toward people or without the motivation to help people learn and grow is, by definition, limiting. The process on which to focus when attempting to boost performance to higher levels is that of bringing out the best in people. The climate factors, the qualities of effective principals, and exceptional teaching themes all emphasize the Peters and Waterman principle, "productivity through people." Our study asserts that the attitudes, decisions, and actions of the professionals working in excellent schools do make a difference in the attainment of quality teaching and learning.

Major Findings and Recommendations

School Climate

Every school climate has a different "feel." It may be cool, comfortable, warm, or just plain empty. Although expressed differently under various circumstances, common climate factors characterize effective schools that form the foundation for achieving student success and measurable educational outcomes.

Order, Purpose, and Coherence. Effective schools possess a sense of order, purpose, direction, and coherence. They are "run" as opposed to merely "running" out of habit. This climate of order common among effective schools generates student achievement, a collective sense of identity, and a sense of decisive purpose. Overall coherence is achieved through clearly articulated goals expressed in a "plan of action" known to the whole organization.

Efficiency and Objectivity. Effective schools contain orderly classrooms where teachers actively organize and plan for efficiency in a quest for more time to spend on instruction and learning. Teachers in achieving schools refuse to waste time and typically hold noninstructional activities to a minimum. From this quest for efficiency springs systematic, objective assessment and continual monitoring of student progress.

Student-centeredness. Effective schools are student-centered. Student needs are given priority over other concerns. An atmosphere of cooperation and trust is created through a high level of interaction between students and teachers. While standardized assessment and careful monitoring of student progess is typical, the daily, face-to-face interaction within effective schools is personal, warm, and supportive. Importance is placed on both academic and nonacademic events that promote student/teacher interaction.

Running somewhat counter to several of the reform recommendations is the emphasis effective schools placed on cocurricular activities that fall into both academic and nonacademic categories. Effective schools do not lose quality in academics by having quality in cocurricular activities. To the contrary, student activities supported by the principal and faculty members create an excitement and school spirit necessary to establishing a positive school climate. While academic learning is considered primary and cocurricular events secondary, effective schools stress the value of student after-school activities that help develop the whole individual and contribute to a unified school culture.

Optimism and High Expectations. Effective schools have a climate of optimism and high expectations. Teachers in high-achieving schools firmly believe that all students can learn and feel responsible for seeing to it that they do. Furthermore, teachers in effective schools believe in their own ability to influence students' learning. In turn, this positive attitude, low sense of futility, and a sense of control are reflected by the students.

Organizational Health. Effective schools possess organizational health. The administrative characteristics contributing to a climate of success are strong leadership, accountability, clear commitment to instructional excellence through inservice education and evaluation, and community involvement.

We believe leaders of schools and school districts could create better educational institutions if they would lend careful attention to and adopt the practices evident in the school climate factors we have defined and discussed throughout our conclusions.

Effective Principals

The principal of a school is the key to its success. We offer the following recommendations as a means for current and future principals to become more effective in guiding and leading schools to high levels of achievement and as criteria for school officials to use when selecting a person to lead a particular school. The same criteria can also serve for subsequent evaluative and developmental purposes.

Because of the vast amount of research on leadership of which our study is but one example, the original belief that leaders are born has changed dramatically over the past four decades. Perhaps there are some inherent characteristics that make some more qualified than others, but most experts agree that many people can learn to be effective leaders. Thus, our findings concerning effective principals not only support prior research, but also have important implications for training and, as mentioned above, for selecting and evaluating school leaders. While different situations may require different behaviors, the following summary of principal characteristics appears to form the foundation for leadership effectiveness. In fact, we have verified to a large extent that these leadership attributes are the generic qualities required to succeed in almost any organizational environment. Furthermore, we believe if these characteristics are developed in present and potential school leaders, educational outcomes and achievement will improve remarkably.

Flexibility in Control

Effective principals are flexible in their approach to leadership and use an appropriate type of control for professionals who have specialized expertise in various areas. They encourage innovation and at the same time tolerate failure. They plan carefully, but they "act now" and do not stifle trial and error. With this "loose-tight" control, they maintain an overall focus on school goals and policies so as to curtail major catastrophes. Teachers are trusted as responsible professionals, and collaborative planning, direction, and order are established and maintained even while important changes and transformations are continually occurring.

Cohesiveness Within the Organization

Effective principals build cohesiveness within the organization by communicating values shared by those within the school. They cultivate cohesiveness through open dialogue and friendly interaction with staff and students. Through a warm interpersonal manner and sincere concern for others, they create unity and pride throughout the school.

Strong Commitment to School Mission

Effective principals have a compelling vision of what their school should look like and be like. They convey an unwavering commitment to the overall school mission through modeling exemplary behavior and communicating their vision. Their commitment helps foster a school culture. As symbolic as well as actual leaders, they are highly visible around the school in a supportive rather than a supervisory role and maintain an "open door."

Recognition and Reward

Effective principals recognize and reward staff accomplishments as well as willingly confront unacceptable performance and behavior. They understand the importance of recognizing success in motivating teachers to become better. Furthermore, they sincerely care about the students and show their concern by stopping students in the hallway for a chat, visiting classrooms to observe firsthand what students are accomplishing, and issuing student awards at assemblies and special ceremonies.

Collaboration and Participation

Effective principals solve problems through collaboration. They are willing to communicate honestly and openly with staff for the purpose of arriving at solutions that work. They see the members of the staff as valuable resources when seeking viable answers for solving conflicts and meeting demands. Collaboration is a routine mode of operation for the best principals especially when developing the overall action plan and curriculum for the school.

Effective Delegation

Effective principals know their staff well and delegate tasks appropriately. They have the ability to match individual strengths with appropriate tasks. Delegation is done clearly and efficiently. Autonomy in getting the job done is granted with minimal supervision. Followup clarifies any confusion and ensures quality of task completion.

Focus on Teaching and Learning

Effective principals care about the quality of teaching and learning that goes on in their schools. In fact, they believe the primary focus on their job is to maintain a focus on delivering the best instruction and learning experiences possible to students. The principal's instructional leadership is critical to the success of the school. Serving as the linkage between schools and external factors, effective principals communicate the importance of the instructional program to the community. Finally, they help both students and faculty focus on achievement through the establishment of schoolwide policies on homework, grading, remediation, progress reports, and retention and promotion, and through careful selection and evaluation of faculty including honest feedback and relevant staff development.

We strongly believe that if these attributes, which appear to lead to success, are cultivated in present and potential principals, the quality of education in schools would show significant and measurable improvement.

Excellent Teachers

Excellent teachers make a difference in the achievements and accomplishments of students and, thus, make a difference in students' lives. Specific attributes have emerged in our study as basic to good teaching. Interestingly, the qualities that constitute excellent teaching appear universal and are not specific to one discipline or subject matter.

Essentially, excellent teachers:

- Are extremely positive, energetic people who are willing to expend more effort in their profession than do average faculty
- Have high expectations of themselves and of their students
- Believe in their students as well as in themselves.

There is little or no sense of futility among excellent teachers nor among the students they teach. A positive regard for all students, not just of good students, generates student success that in turn rewards the teacher. This cycle of high expectation, success, reward, and motivation appears to be a key factor that keeps excellent teachers in the profession.

As with leadership attributes, certain inherent characteristics may make some teachers more qualified than others, but most individuals can learn to be effective. Clearly, commitment or the desire to be a good teacher is a cornerstone to excellent teaching. We offer the following summary recommendations as guidelines for improvement to teachers already in classrooms and to potential teachers. These qualities can also serve as criteria for training and selecting good teachers. Master or lead teachers should be chosen on the basis of these characteristics. Furthermore, administrators can link assessment, evaluation, motivation, reward, and development to the characteristics identified in our study.

Teacher Motivating Themes

Strong Commitment

Excellent teachers demonstrate strong commitment in their belief that all students can learn and that they as teachers have the ability to promote that learning. Thus, they believe in their own efficacy as well as feel responsible for providing the means for learning. They model task-orientation and project a serious regard for the learning process. In addition, they are friendly yet businesslike in attitude. Excellent teachers expect students to accomplish realistic but challenging goals and make students accountable for their own learning. By taking this position, they make students aware that their performance results from their own efforts. Finally, excellent teachers are accessible both in and outside of class for extra assistance to both remedial and advanced students when needed, and they are actively involved in cocurricular activities.

Goal Orientation

Effective teachers set goals in their own lives and in their classes, exhibiting a strong sense of direction both personally and professionally.

Integrated Perception

Excellent teachers view students and their teaching holistically. They see themselves teaching students rather than subjects and see students as whole individuals operating in a broader context beyond the classroom. Exceptional teachers are aware of students' abilities, interests, problems, and needs. They help students learn how to learn, to think, and to problem solve as opposed to having them memorize particular facts and subject matter details. Integrated perception exhibited by the best teachers provides unity and continuity to daily lessons and further develops an understanding in students of how facts and concepts fit into a larger context.

Reward Orientation

Excellent teachers are motivated by, perhaps more than anything else, the satisfaction they receive from the successes and accomplishments of their students. This satisfaction is heightened when students, parents, and administrators express their appreciation of teachers and of their critical role in helping students to achieve.

Teacher Interpersonal Themes

Objectivity

Excellent teachers use appropriate discipline techniques. They include carefully patterned routines that focus on behavior rather than on individuals and prevent disruption before it begins. They have excellent monitoring skills and know what is going on in the classroom at all times. If disruption does occur, excellent teachers act quickly to foster learning and reduce time off-task. They remain task-oriented and in control of the class and of themselves, and they are unwilling to let one individual disrupt the learning of the whole class for very long. Exercising a methodical approach to classroom management and discipline, effective teachers look for causes rather than blame, gather facts, confer privately and quietly with transgressors, and explore alternatives with students for changing unacceptable behavior. Finally, they clearly communicate expected behavior to students, inform them of the consequences of disruptive actions, and demonstrate fair treatment.

Active Listening

Excellent teachers are excellent listeners. They reveal sincere interest in students and what they have to say through active listening. Also, excellent teachers check students' comprehension by using interchangeable techniques of active listening such as acceptance, paraphrasing, and pausing to allow time for answering. They sense the mood of the class through attention to nonverbal cues and attend to informal talk as well as formal class discussions.

Rapport and Empathy

Excellent teachers build good rapport with students and are able to empathize with them. They establish harmonious, warm, supportive classrooms by showing respect for students, treating them fairly, and trusting them. By modeling expected behavior, they set the expectation that students will respect the teacher as well as one another. Exceptional secondary teachers understand the thoughts and emotions of their teenage students who are undergoing dramatic personal changes.

Teacher Cognitive Themes

Individualized Perception

Excellent teachers find out about their students as individuals, diagnose their needs objectively, and then incorporate that knowledge into the planned instructional activities. They recognize effort and improvement as well as superior performance. They work harder for low-achievers, using more patience, persistence, diagnosis, and remediation. They capitalize on student interests and work to personalize instruction.

Teaching Strategies

Excellent teachers are skillful, enthusiastic, well-organized, student-centered, accurately evaluative, flexible, and clever at getting students involved. Through a variety of teaching strategies, executed skillfully and enthusiastically, they activate students to think, respond, learn, and grow. With meticulous planning and preparation, they maximize the amount of time spent on instruction and learning. Furthermore, excellent teachers think all the way through a lesson and plan for the expected and the unexpected. Even after preparing in advance, they remain flexible, ready to incorporate occurrences relevant to the lesson into the plan. Expectations, criteria, and objectives are made clear at the beginning of a course and of each lesson. Excellent teachers generally exhibit a student-centered style as opposed to teacher- or subject-centered. The curriculum is developed to meet the needs of the students rather than to reflect the teacher's specialty or preferences. Excellent teachers give specific praise and corrective feedback. They involve students by using variety, thus forestalling boredom. Exceptional teachers recognize that getting students involved is a critical variable to effective teaching and learning. For the best teachers, no two days are ever alike.

Knowledge

Excellent teachers have sound knowledge of both their subject matter and teaching techniques. They perceive themselves as learners and constantly engage in professional and personal development activities.

Innovation

Excellent teachers search unrelentingly for new and current information and then work systematically to incorporate worthwhile innovations into their classrooms. They describe themselves as risk-takers and are willing to change anything that is not working or to improve and upgrade existing programs that are already successful. Staying current in their field, whether in their subject matter or in education in general, is important to them. They actively seek ways to renew and enliven their approach as well as work to make their classes relevant and up-to-date.

General Recommendations

Recommending a longer school day and year misses the mark somewhat. From our observation, most of the time available is not very well used. Good teachers use the available time well and achieve good results. Thus, extending time in school is not an answer; better use of time is. Teachers with the attributes we have identified should be recognized and rewarded and held as models from whom others can learn.

And although structure and regulation are necessary to building a sound educational system, we must remember that *good* teachers who are engaged in daily classroom interaction probably know better how to teach than those further up in the hierarchy. Therefore, control over educational practices ought to be appropriate, lending broad parameters when establishing what should be accomplished, such as goals, objectives, and competencies. Structure should also allow professionals who are well-trained in their areas plenty of room to use their unique personalities and draw on their own resources to motivate individuals through the learning process. This recommendation calls for greater trust and respect for teachers' opinions and for increased involvement of teachers in the overall decision process whether it relates to choosing textbooks or establishing outcome criteria.

Conclusion

The attributes we have identified that describe successful principals and teachers have important implications for selection and hiring, staff development, and programs in higher education that prepare administrators and teachers. The professional achieving excellence under the adverse conditions in public education today have powerfully positive outlooks and have refused to bow to obstacles; they present an image of educators that is worthy of respect and reverence. We feel their stories are worth telling. These profiles may serve as guides for training future educators and for developing those already in our educational system.

We agree with the reformist authors that public education in America has been in serious trouble. But we know that excellence already exists in many schools, and we believe that identifying, developing, and rewarding behaviors associated with excellence can promote quality in education. We contend that the attributes identified in our study as characterizing excellence in principals and teachers can be developed.

Clearly, some characteristics appear more teachable than others. However, through tremendous strides accomplished by research in recent decades, we have learned specific ways in which to help individuals develop into effective leaders and teachers.

How can we teach the reward that teachers feel when a student succeeds after a long struggle? This feeling of reward motivates teachers. What if a person is not moved by another's achievement? Can this person be an excellent teacher? Perhaps, but without empathy for others, it would not be easy. Therefore, competencies that can be taught and developed should be, and the inner qualities that appear necessary for achieving excellence should be modeled by individuals who have them. Possibly, awareness of these apparently inherent qualities can inspire others to recognize those same inner attributes within themselves.

Furthermore, the models we have presented may assist those who select and hire educators to identify the qualities that appear fundamental to the personality of excellent educators. Those who prepare and train educators may work toward developing potential qualities specifically known to characterize excellence. The first step in this developmental process is to identify what it is that exceptional educators do. Once agreement is reached, standards of quality may be established. Because our study supports much of the research about effective teaching and administering, we believe agreement is imminent. The key to this agreement is people. Good programs do not necessarily make for good schools, but people do. Our goals in this study has been to discover how people create excellent schools.

Our results confirm Ted Sizer's view that effective schools are the result of "good kid people"—adults who can easily engage and inspire students. In virtually any setting, these "kid people" are able to connect on a personal basis with any group of students and help them to achieve clear, meaningful goals. We can easily describe the participants in our study, principals and teachers alike, as "kid people." Their action is directly related to creating a purposeful, orderly school climate in which real learning occurs. We believe that the subjects in our research offer superb models for the way effective schools should be organized and managed. Implementing and emulating these models provides a clear means for bringing excellence to education.

CHAPTER II
SCHOOL CLIMATE

A school's climate—the overall environment, values, shared beliefs, and personality—clearly affects the inhabitants of the school.

When meteorologists use the term climate, they refer to the prevailing, continuous pattern of elements, such as aridity or high humidity. Minor details, for example, rainfall or barometric pressure, are part of a climate only as they contribute to a consistent pattern.

When we speak of an organizational climate, we are typically commenting how much we may like or dislike a place, or the extent to which the place is hospitable to life, comfort, and growth. An arid climate, after all, is not likely to be lush and inviting, and neither is an arctic one. Climate, then, is typically linked in our minds with life, growth, and productivity. So it is with the climate of school buildings or school districts. Some are arctic, some are arid, and some are conducive to growth—academic, physical, or emotional—of the people who inhabit them.

Organizations, be they as large as General Motors or as small as an elementary school, have organizational climates. It only takes a few visits to any school to notice its unique "feel." One school seems oppressive and joyless; another seems vital and alive; and a third school merely feels empty. This "feel" is the school's climate—a result of daily decisions made by those in charge of the learning environment. This climate makes the difference between the success or failure of the school and its students.

Do we know then what kind of climate makes for an effective school? Unfortunately, there does not appear to be a formula, and we cannot point to any *single* factor as a predictor of high levels of student success—for example, high scores on national tests. Schools represent incredibly complex environments. From previous studies and our own we can identify several characteristics common to a large majority of effective schools. These variables surface as *common denominators* of student and school success.

Order, Purpose, and Coherence

First, research indicates that schools effective in inspiring achievement in their students possess a sense of order, purpose, direction, and coherence. Underlying this sense of order is the immediate impression that effective schools are "'being run' as opposed to 'running,'" according to a study by the Center of Educational Research and Development (1978). Moreover, as Gilbert Austin expressed it, effective schools possess a climate of purposefulness; that is, they operate with a sense of purpose rather than simply out of habit (1979, pp. 10-14). Similarly, George Weber's study of inner city schools found that "it is difficult to escape the conviction that the order, sense of purpose, relative quiet, and pleasure in learning of these schools play a role in their achievement" (1971, p. 26).

Researchers report that:

- Effective schools are characteristically quiet and clean, with a positive physical appearance
- The physical plant shows little evidence of vandalism
- Repairs to the physical plant show evidence of being completed promptly, preserving a cared-for appearance.

Order and purpose are obviously highly valued. This pervasive sense of order does not occur by accident, but by intent and action. Order is achieved with a network of rules that are clear, reasonable, fair, and consistently enforced, creating a climate of pride and responsibility. Richard J. Gigliotti and Wilbur B. Brookover assert that a substantial network of rules and policies, combined with consistent and continuous reinforcement, works to "minimize confusion" and to generate a "sense of control" (1975, pp. 245-261). Also, continuous review of policies updates the rules. Throughout the school there is uniform understanding of the school system's prohibitions and punishments (Wynne, 1981, pp. 377-381).

The consequence of this climate of order and purpose is what William Georgiades (1978) termed "a humane institution," a place where students have a sense of a collective identity that is fostered daily by the school's unique climate (Wynne, 1981). This sense of identity is further cultivated by conspicuous recognition of student accomplishments, through the use of honor societies, award assemblies, school paper notices, and pins, accompanied by the use of school mottos, colors, and symbols.

Another element of an effective school climate is a coherent plan. As Edward A. Wynne notes, the entire school community—

administrators, teachers, students, and parents—have a common set of concepts, know the school's goals and objectives, and can subsequently act in "a coherent fashion" (1981). Many other researchers have noted that effective schools have a common denominator, they all have a shared "plan of action."

The master plan is not simply a document written to satisfy the district administration. It is a working document that guides the daily behavior of the teachers and administrators who wrote it. Moreover, the goals are reinforced at staff meetings and in classrooms. The end product is a continuously developed instructional program, which, according to Richard L. Venezky and Linda F. Winfield (1979), in itself, contributes to an overall sense of order and purpose. There are few fits and starts, few ill-fated ventures into instructional innovation, and few educational mistakes. What happens is what was planned to happen, with few embarrassing errors.

When studying the climates of our participating schools, we examined data previously collected by the United States Department of Education (ED) and used to determine each school's eligibility for nomination as an excellent school in the 1982-83 Secondary School Recognition Program. Of the 154 award winning schools, 39 sent us the ED information that we have used to evaluate school climate. However, 54 schools participated in the overall study by responding to the openended questionnaires about teachers and principals from which we have extracted the principal and teacher characteristics. In other words, not all participating schools, for one reason or another, sent the ED information.

After comparing our sample to brief school profiles (abstracted from the ED data taken from the entire set of 154 schools) it appears that the sample for which we have complete data is representative of the entire group. Of the 39 schools that sent complete ED data, 69 percent are high schools and 31 percent are junior or middle schools. Among these schools, school district size ranges from 1,337 to 350,000. Fifty-nine percent of the schools are rural, 31 percent urban, and 10 percent suburban. Also, the schools have an ethnic mix with some schools having up to 50 percent black students and others as many as 72 percent Hispanic. The population of white students in the schools ranges from 18 to 99 percent, with a mean of 56 percent. The percentage of students coming from low income families attending these schools ranges from 1 to 70, with a mean of 16 percent. All in all, the schools receiving recognition for outstanding quality represent a good cross-section of school types, sizes, socioeconomic status, and ethnic composition.

Although the schools differ and, therefore, reflect climate factors in different ways, the data show that these schools have many of the same characteristics reflected in literature on school climate. For instance, a sense of order, purpose, and coherence prevails among the schools—they establish clear academic goals and well-articulated curricula. Furthermore, they are led by strong principals who generally use specific, concrete strategies to emphasize and work toward increased time on academic learning. Finally, in the schools, the principals and faculties recognize and reward student achievement and effort.

Efficiency and Objectivity

The next major set of characteristics singled out by researchers as common to effective schools pertains to the *classroom environment*. First, the climate within the classrooms conveys a sense of *efficiency*, a sense that the classrooms have been organized to create more time for instruction and to avoid the waste of time that is typical of ineffective schools (Wynne, 1981). In fact, some researchers find that in effective schools as much as 80 percent of the time available to teachers is spent on instruction (for example, see the Office of Program Evaluation and Research, 1977). In almost all cases, teachers have actively organized for efficiency seeking to spend more time on instruction (Berliner, 1982).

Essentially, the teachers *organize* the classrooom for efficiency. They actively control the environment to produce results in their students. These teachers and students view time as a precious commodity and refuse to waste it. Noninstructional activities are held to a minimum. (More discussion on teachers' contributions to creating an appropriate school climate appears in Chapter 4).

Similarly, researchers found that the quest for efficiency resulted in *systematic, objective assessments*. Not surprisingly, effective schools tend to rely on objective test results rather than subjective "teacher recommendations" when placing students in classes or when evaluating their progress, according to the *California School Effectiveness Study* by the Office of Program Evaluation and Research (1977), and others (Vallina, 1970; Fetters et al., 1968).

Rather than viewing such actions as depersonalizing, the teachers in effective schools consider systematic assessment as necessary to cultivating student success. Also, effective schools tend to have an environment that accepts *continual monitoring* of student progress. All are aware of their latest test scores, their academic progress, and their poor performances. Moreover, the data are used, not simply recorded. The results help determine the curriculum, the teachers' goals, and whether or not a student receives special help. In fact, continual monitoring takes place on a minute-by-minute basis. Correct answers are praised, incorrect answers are identified, and students with difficulties receive immediate help.

Student-Centeredness

What exactly does student centeredness mean? Many school climate studies report that school personnel focused on student needs and worked cooperatively to meet these needs. The teachers

- Better understand the special characteristics of their students
- Use a variety of materials for different students at the same time
- Attempt to "integrate the cultural background of the students with school learning" (New York Office of Education Performance Review, 1974)
- Modify the curricular design, the text selections, and the teaching strategies to respond to individual students (Edmonds, 1978).

Also, teachers frequently group students by ability within the single classroom to enable them to give special attention to the variety of skill levels they have within classes. The willingness to modify classroom environment, the curriculum, and instructional strategies to help individual students progress is often cited as characteristic of outstanding schools, says the Phi Delta Kappa study, "Why Do Some Urban Schools Succeed?" (1980). Taken together, they indicate that students' needs are given priority over the concerns of others.

Student-centeredness is also expressed in another way: There exists a *high level of interaction between students and teachers*. As Austin notes, teachers in effective schools strive to be warmer and more emotionally responsive to their students (1979). They know their students by name, and have close, advisory relationships with them (Georgiades, 1978). This, in turn, creates an atmosphere of cooperation and trust between students and teachers. Impersonality and objectivity may be typical of the standardized assessment of student progress, but the daily, face-to-face interaction within effective schools is universally personal, warm, supportive, and close. Not surprisingly, teachers with "high interpersonal skills" have students who are absent less, who achieve higher, and who create fewer discipline problems (Aspy and Roebuck, 1974). Moreover, exemplary schools actually *plan* for such interaction, by scheduling both academic and nonacademic events that will promote student-teacher interaction (Fonstad, 1973). The end result is a warm, open climate where students are known by the teachers personally, and where students have the opportunity to interact frequently and closely with their teachers.

Student-centeredness clearly exists in the school in our study and typifies the operating style of effective schools. In these schools individual differences are taken into account in the planning and implementation of programs. Student response and participation are serious goals in the majority of the sample schools that offer bilingual and multicultural programs. Interestingly, and yet not surprisingly, these schools emphasize both academic and nonacademic cocurricular activities that help build school spirit. Although contrary to several of the reform recommendations, limiting or abolishing participation in clubs, teams, and various other after-school groups in order to free up more time for academic learning indeed detracts from the unified school culture and would eliminate some unique learning opportunities. The large majority of our effective schools stress the importance of cocurricular functions and the variety of learning activities they provide. However, all participants in our study quickly point out the importance of keeping academic learning primary and cocurricular events secondary. Furthermore, we would speculate that if these alternative and supplemental learning opportunities were eliminated altogether, the resulting void would likely diminish the effectiveness of these schools.

Optimism and High Expectations

A fourth major variable found by researchers is the climate of optimism and high expectations that permeates the classrooms of outstanding schools. This is not just a simple hope that all will achieve to their potential. Instead, it is a *conviction* held by both the student and teachers that classrooms are an environment where success is inevitable. Teachers in effective schools do not believe that students are permanently scarred by race, poverty, or social status. Typically they believe strongly that, within the climate of their particular classroom, the student can learn (Brundage, 1980).

The research-based evidence for this attitude is overwhelming, leading to the conclusion that this climate of optimism is indispensable if students are to achieve. Indeed, more than just being optimistic about the students' ability to learn, the teachers often express a belief that they are responsible for seeing that their students perform at higher levels, an attitude frequently lacking at other, less effective schools. This belief extends throughout the entire school climate, affecting all.

This climate of optimism has other, equally interesting dimensions. For example, the teachers themselves believe that they can influence students to learn. They have a lower level of pessimism concerning their ability to influence their students and less of a tendency to blame students, parents, or other external factors for poor student performance (New York Office of Education Performance Review, 1974). In other words, the teachers generally have an *internal locus of control;* they see that success or failure is a consequence of what they did. Luck, they felt, had little to do with how their students performed in class (Armor et al., 1976).

Likewise, students seem to share in this climate of optimism, gaining from it *a positive attitude, a low sense of futility,* and *a sense of control* over the learning tasks and activities. All three of these student attitudes have been shown to be vitally important to the success of students. As Brookover found in his research, a low sense of academic futility is the climate variable most often present in outstanding schools (Brookover and Lezotte, 1979). Much like their teachers, high-achieving students seldom attribute their success or failure to luck, exhibiting the same sense of control as their teachers (Center of Educational Research and Development, 1978). In fact, many studies indicate that this sense of control bears the greatest relationship with student achievement.

Repeatedly shown to be crucial to student success, the climate of optimism exists not by accident but by design. It starts with a fundamental belief among teachers that all students are educable, with no excuses allowed. This is then coupled with an optimism on the teacher's part that he or she is able to make a difference in whether or not the student succeeds. Indeed, this optimism is often present as a sense of personal responsibility for the student's success. Communicated daily to the students, they soon internalize this sense of optimism and commitment, transforming it into a personal sense of control over how well they learn.

Existing, perhaps as a side effect of this optimism, is another characteristic of effective schools: *an atmosphere of high expectation for students' academic development.* Numerous researchers found that the professional staff in effective schools tends to predict higher educational accomplishments for their pupils, and the teachers generally expect more students to graduate from high school and college. Also, in the classroom, everyone concerned has high expectations that the learning objectives will be achieved. In fact, as Mary R. Hoover found, "it is assumed that teachers can teach and that they want to teach" (1978, p. 757). High expectations exist for both students and teachers.

In our schools, high expectations and optimism stand out as distinct characteristics. The teachers firmly believe that they can and do make a difference in students' learning, and, therefore, in their lives. We have labelled this conviction "teacher efficacy." Closely related to this concept is the positive regard of the teachers for students. They sincerely believe their students can achieve and learn. (Further elaboration on these characteristics appears in subsequent chapters.)

Organizational Health

Another key ingredient of the climate of effective schools is its health as an organization. As mentioned earlier, organizations, like the people that work in them, have personalities; and it is the personality of the school as a professional organization that often makes a difference to those who work and learn there. Researchers have identified several administrative characteristics of effective schools. These characteristics profile an organization with strong leadership, accountability, clear commitment to instructional excellence through inservice education and evaluation, and community involvement.

First, it has been found that successful schools feel they are being led, not merely managed. A caretaker approach to administration appears to be out of place in these schools. They are run, not simply running. The leadership comes primarily from the school principal, who is consistently viewed as a source of strong leadership, direction, and support. The principal clearly expresses behavioral expectations of the staff, creating a clear understanding of organizational goals. Also, principals in effective schools are well-organized, task-oriented, and well-informed about what is happening throughout the school. In fact, these principals spend most of their days outside of their offices.

Typically these principals have high expectations for themselves, the teaching staff, and the students of their school. They exert pressure for this high achievement on all those around them, encourage professionalism and initiative among the staff, are directly involved at all levels of the school, and communicate a sense of positive leadership.

Second, research frequently finds that these principals perceive themselves as instructional leaders and exercise this leadership role more often than principals of less effective schools. Numerous researchers record that principals in effective schools are heavily involved in instruction. The New York Education Performance Review (1974) noted that these principals are "quietly omnipresent," making formal and informal observations of the faculty and staff. High visibility seems to be the benchmark of these organizational climates. Also, the principals assume that their leadership commits them to monitoring and observing the use of classroom time (Lipham, 1981), and to evaluating the achievement of organizational goals and the basic learning objectives (Brookover and Lezottte, 1979).

It is important to note that this instructional leadership of the principal seldom displaces the teacher's similar role. In fact, many research studies show that this commitment to leadership felt by the principal is typically coupled to a commitment to participative decision making. This simply means that the principal provides for staff input into school decision, creating a "positive atmosphere and a feeling of ownership of decisions made affecting the school" (Phi Delta Kappa, 1980). Decision making is shared throughout the organization; and the responsibility for planning, implementation, and evaluation is likewise shared among members of the professional staff.

Third, the organizational climate of these successful schools is growth-oriented. The organization is committed to the professional growth of its employees, especially its teachers, through inservice education programs. As Russell Gersten discovered, the organization's efforts at "linking teachers with efficacious assistance" is a crucial step toward excellence for schools (Gersten et al., 1982). Also, such excellence is often connected to the teachers' perception of inservice education as a source of growth, rather than as a waste of time (Armor et al., 1976). Similarly, teachers in exemplary schools are committed to staff development programs that are closely tied to the instructional program (Office of Program Evaluation and Research, 1980). Finally, the teachers frequently involve themselves in running staff development efforts, encouraging the exchange of ideas, and giving clear priority to the classroom carry-over from inservice programs (Vallina, 1970).

Fourth, the organizational climate is imbued with a sense of professional accountability through evaluation. In practical terms, this means that the teachers in successful schools welcome systematic efforts to evaluate their teaching effectiveness, both by their peers and by the administration. This seems to be a logical extension of the climate of accountability and responsibility that teachers feel for student success. As Hoover notes, teachers, as well as students, are expected to achieve, grow, and be successful (1978). The concept of accountability, then, is not limited to students. Instead, it is reflected throughout the professional organization, conveying to all involved that success is the goal and that progress toward that goal will be monitored.

Fifth, the professional working climate within an effective school encourages an awareness and an acceptance of the community in which it exists. Many researchers point out that good schools have good reputations. They are aware of whom they serve, whose children have been entrusted to them, and whose goodwill they receive. These schools characteristically have more active PTA's, higher levels of parent-initiated involvement, more parents who visit classrooms, and principals who report having better rapport with parents. Also, within successful schools, both students and staff members are encouraged to participate in collective community projects. The question of whether successful schools have a better community rapport and reputation because they are unusually successful, or if these schools are successful because they are in touch with the community does not have a clear answer. However, successful schools do know their community; they cultivate a rapport with their community and work hard to gain their reputations.

Organizational health is also an earmark of the schools we have studied. Because the principals' leadership characteristics and teachers' qualities are so crucial to overall climate, they are developed in subsequent chapters. The actions and behaviors of the people within a school are the elements comprising the climate, not shiny gadgets and new furniture. The principals in our study contribute to organizational health through strong leadership, staff involvement, systematic evaluation of instruction, and rewarding and recognizing their faculty and staff. Strong community support and involvement are other signs of organizational health.

Taken together, these five organizational characteristics of the outstanding, exemplary schools—strong leadership at the top, a strong instructional thrust, a strong growth orientation, a strong sense of accountability, and a strong commitment to community relations—all combine to create a truly professional atmosphere for the employees. They see the school as a professional workplace where they have strong, directive leadership, where they must be committed to their own evaluation, and where they must always welcome the advice and complaints of the people they serve.

In conclusion, it should be apparent that the climate common to the many effective schools across the country is an amazingly complex one. Nonetheless, what the many research studies (including our own) into effective schools have found is that there are certain characteristics associated with the climate within these excellent schools: order, purpose, coherence, efficiency, objectivity, student centeredness, optimism, an atmosphere of high expectations, and a certain administrative healthiness. Each of these characteristics contributes to a climate that is hospitable to success, achievement, and growth.

CHAPTER III
EFFECTIVE PRINCIPALS

Agreement is widespread—the principal of a school is the key to its success. All of the factors commonly associated with school effectiveness relate, directly or indirectly, to principal effectiveness, according to a study by A. Lorri Manasse in *Principal,* March 1982. The school principal—the most visible, "on-line" administrator— serves as a pivotal exchange point, a working broker between teachers, students, parents, the superintendent, the school board, and others (Crowson and Porter-Gehrie, 1981).

Throughout the literature, some behaviors and functions show up over and over as characteristics of excellent principals. And while we don't offer them as a recipe, because different situations may require different behaviors, we do believe that most effective principals address these characteristics as the basis for their effectiveness.

Many educators, including principals themselves, see the principal's job as extremely complex, ambiguous, and stressful. Leadership theory offers a number of possible styles to describe principal behavior, but virtually everyone who writes about principal behaviors says "it depends on the situation." So contingency theorists offer ways to analyze the situation and respond to it. Principals often feel frustrated because they aren't sure what their roles are and/or because there is an increasing gap between how they believe they should spend their time and how they do (Manasse, 1982).

Schools today reflect their complex environments. Yet many principals continue to view leadership as either an authoritarian role (a management link in the chain of command) or as a democratic role (with participative decision making), according to Raphael O. Nystrand's article, "Leadership Theories for Principals" (1981). Others feel their choice is between being a manager of resources who allows considerable autonomy to teachers and maintains stability, or being an instructional leader who is active in pushing changes in teacher behavior and classroom programs, says Judith Warren Little in "The Effective Principal" (1982). The solution seems to be that all of these views are appropriate to certain situations.

Principals' tasks are numerous and varied, and several studies have shown that principals move quickly from task to task and are frequently interrupted. Therefore, they have little time for "prolonged contemplation" because they must make decisions on the spot (Blumberg and Greenfield, 1980). Much of their time is spent on complex management tasks. There are frequently no criteria for hiring principals, nor does central staff provide criteria after a new principal is hired. But many principals think (or believe that central office thinks) that one of their major functions is to maintain stability.

Gary Yukl, in *The Effective Principal: A Research Summary*, names the functions of principals as most important:

- Develop goals, policies, and directions
- Organize the school and develop programs to accomplish the goals
- Monitor progress, solve problems, and maintain order
- Procure, manage, and allocate resources
- Create a climate for personal and professional growth and development
- Represent the school to the district office and the outside community.

By virtue of their position, principals have certain "rights of initiative." They can stimulate, sustain, or alter expectations for performance in ways that others cannot. They can shape the job to their own liking by choosing to spend more time and energy on one aspect of the job than on others. Some principals focus on teachers and the instructional program, others on things that have a definite payoff (such as materials or special events), others on "law enforcements" (discipline, counseling), and others on quasi-political interests (high visibility with the community and local politicians). None can completely ignore any of these factors, but they can choose the areas they want to emphasize.

One of the key maintenance functions is to maintain disciplinary stability. Learning cannot take place in a school that is chaotic, unsafe, and heavily vandalized. Order provides an opportunity for teaching and learning. Principals use different styles, of course, and some routine disciplinary management may be delegated to others. But most principals tour, say William J. Martin and Donald J. Willower in "The Managerial Behavior of High School Principals" (1981). They try to anticipate and prevent problems and stop them by being in the halls between classes, in the cafeteria at lunch, at the on-campus bus stops and recreation areas, and generally around the building. On these tours, they can stop little problems. They work to control any crises that do occur. They develop and enforce policies and rules. They work to maintain an image of order and cleanliness. And they model appropriate behaviors. Much of this work is done on the spot; the principal's presence, reminders, enforcement, and modeling serve to make expectations clear about behavior in the school.

Teachers and principals participating in our research cite "modeling expected behavior" as a concrete means by which a principal conveys purpose and gains cooperation. The following excerpt by Deborah Cheryl Courter, a teacher at Prospect Heights, provides some evidence of how expectations are communicated through the principal's presence and modeling.

> Because of his vision to make Prospect Heights Middle School the best middle school in the state, it has become so. He was able to accomplish this by his fine qualities of leadership. He sets the example not only in personal appearance, but also in caring for others. As a result, the whole atmosphere of the school is one of cooperation, helpfulness, and high standards.

Another key function of the principal is working with the external environment or "keeping 'outside' forces under control." One study lists three ways to do this.

- The first is by protecting the work of the school. Effective principals use the community to provide resources, support, and information.

- The second is by building community support. They initiate communication and often use their discretionary power in granting a special request from a parent.

- Third, they orchestrate community involvement by combining parent involvement in the school with little real power, because of the need to maintain stability without "outside" interference (Crowson and Porter-Gehrie, 1981, p. 34).

Our study results suggest that effective principals believe one of their major functions is to protect teachers from outside interference. W. Terrence Hannon, principal of Taft Middle School in New Mexico, writes:

> Teachers are to teach. The administration attempts to eliminate or take care of other non-teaching activities.... The staff is asked to undertake only those tasks that are related to the school....We do not ask staff to do someone

else's or my busy work. It is the principal's responsibility to prevent this from occurring.

In spite of the ambiguity and complexity inherent in the role of today's educational leader, some principals are successful at becoming effective leaders. What is effective varies from one situation to another, of course. Several studies have identified two or more leadership "styles." Researchers at the Research and Development Center at the University of Texas have named three common styles—the *responder*, the *manager*, and the *initiator*. K.A. Leithwood and D.J. Montgomery (1982) discuss "effective" and "typical" principals. Others simply note that there is a variety of styles. What is important is the match between the style and the situation, says Wynn De Bevoise in "Synthesis of Research on the Principal as Instructional Leader" (1984).

• *Responders* allow others to take the lead. They see their primary task as running a smooth school in which teachers and students are reasonably content. Because they emphasize personal relationships, they listen to others a lot or let them make the decisions, and they consider teachers as strong professionals who need little guidance. There is little evidence of vision or long-range planning in the responder (Hall et al, 1984).

• *Managers* are responsive to situations or people, and they also initiate actions to support change. They are sensitive to teachers, they keep them informed, and they buffer staff from outside interference or excessive demands. They do not initiate action beyond the basics of what is imposed (Hall et al, 1984).

• *Initiators* are pushers. They have clear, decisive, long-term goals. They have very strong beliefs about what the school could be, and they work intensely to attain their vision. They have high expectations, they monitor closely, and they make decisions based on what they think is best for the school, even if those decisions don't make everybody happy (Hall et al, 1984).

Gene Hall and his colleagues summarize these three styles in "Leadership Variables Associated with Successful School Improvement" (1983):

> Initiators make it happen.
> Managers help it happen.
> Responders let it happen.

These are not the only styles, of course. Hall et al. suggest "despot," "covert saboteur," and "guerilla" as other possibilities.

And no one fits these three stereotypes precisely. The terms are more like points on a continuum, and a principal may move on the continuum as the situation warrants (Hall et al., 1983, 1984).

Other research also says that effective principals are initiators who "assume a proactive stance toward their job situation. They [do] not allow themselves to become bogged down in 'administrivia'" (Blumberg and Greenfield, 1980, p. 205). These principals push assertively to make things happen. Hall uses the term "change facilitator" because many of the characteristics of effective instructional leadership and good principals are directly related to the facilitation of change (Hall et al., 1983). Effective principals stir things up; they are not content with maintaining the status quo (De Bevoise, 1984; Snyder, 1984). They have a high energy level and are willing to work to make things happen (Yukl, 1982).

Virtually none of the principals participating in our study could be classified as responders. Many are excellent managers but also exhibit qualities going far beyond the managerial level. Clearly, the large majority of the principals in our study are initiators who take action and set long-term goals. They communicate their goals to the staff and are actively involved at all levels of school operations. The following example, written by Marjorie Ratliff, a teacher at Lake Oswego High School, describing her principal, illustrates strong initiating orientation as opposed to merely management-directed or reaction-driven behavior:

> Mr. Korach reduces the number of interruptions due to activities through careful planning and has the courage to make changes. He conveys high expectations of us through the way he speaks with us and through written building goals. He conducts his own class, Humanities, in a manner that says he is serious about learning.
> He asserts the authority of his position by making decisions in a timely, efficient manner. He does not back away from confrontations with students, faculty, or parents. His commitment to his job is evident.

One of the most common observations in the literature is that the role of the principal varies with the situation. Yukl describes six sets of school variables that can affect a principal's role: elementary/secondary, large/small, urban/rural, new/established, public/private, and stressful (strikes, RIF, vandalism, and so on)/normal maintenance (1982). What is effective in one situation may not be appropriate in another. Principals do not act in isolation. They must consider many factors, both internal and external, that affect a given

situation. Not everyone is a superstar; most peope are strong in one
or two areas, weak in others. The key to making a diversity of styles
work is to match the appropriate style with the situation. Many
studies indicate, as does James Lipham in *Effective Principal, Effective
School,* that "some principals become firmly wedded to a particular
style (for example, directiveness or supportiveness) rather than
develop the ability to shift their styles as circumstances warrant"
(1981). Flexibility is better, but few people can change their whole
style, although they can change certain behaviors.

Nystrand points out that while the best principals are high on
task and human relations scales, not all leaders are equally adept or
even so inclined. And both kinds of behavior are not equally important in a given situation. The problem is deciding which style to use
when. Thus is born contingency theory. Nystrand summarizes
Fiedler's contingency theory, Vroom and Yetton's decision-making
model, and the Path/Goal theory of Evans and House (1981).

Fielder's theory uses a scale to determine the Least Preferred
Coworker (LPC). While the method is somewhat complicated,
studies show that people with a low LPC are task-oriented; they
work better in situations that are very favorable (clear task, interpersonal relations, a strong power base) or very unfavorable. Principals with a high LPC are people-oriented and work better with a
middle situation. According to this theory, everyone has a basic
style, implying that leaders should try to understand their own
styles and seek situations that match. However, Nystrand warns
that there is much disagreement about the LPC measures and
whether the style or the situation can or should be changed.

The Vroom-Yetton model is based on a taxonomy of decision-
making modes. The leader chooses a decision-making style—for
example, authoritarian, consultive, participative—based on the
situation and on what the leader wants to achieve—for example,
decision, quality, subordinate acceptance, time efficiency. This
theory is also somewhat based on contingency. The problem lies in
the leader's ability to determine the appropriate mode.

Evans and House's Path-Goal theory assumes that leader
behavior has its most direct effect on a subordinate's psychological
state. So a leader tries to provide motivation or satisfaction. The
leader's behavior is determined by the situation, but his or her basic
function is to clarify subordinates' goals and ease their path toward
achieving those goals.

While there are several ways that leaders can help subordinates
reach their goals (such as reducing barriers to the goal or helping the
subordinate clarify expectations), the key is understanding the par-

ticular needs of individuals in given situations. If the relationship between the path and the goal is already clear, then the leader's efforts are not appreciated. Thus, a teacher may resent close monitoring, "teacher-proof" curriculum, or a request to provide input into self-evident decisions. All three of these theories—Fiedler's contingency theory, the Vroom-Yetton model, and Path-Goal theory—reflect situation-specific variables. Principals must determine how to judge the situation, how to act within it, and how to judge themselves. Donald Mackenzie, in the April 1983 issue of *Educational Researcher*, summarizes the situation:

> In this environment, nothing works all the time. Almost anything that makes sense will work more often than not, if it is implemented with enough self-critical optimism and zest. Some things work more often than others, but hardly anything works for everybody. Nothing works by itself, and everything takes a long time.

Knowing the right people to call on in a given situation stands out as a strength and a general motif among the behaviors of principals in our study who head high-achieving schools. The leader's ability to be flexible and to alter approaches depending on the circumstances is illustrated in these examples, written by teachers about their principals:

> Mr. Ritchie is acutely aware of teacher strengths and uses them for different situations. He knows which teachers relate well to which groups of students (Chester Chase, Katahdin High School in Maine, describing Principal Loren Ritchie).

> Terry knows his faculty. He has taken time during and after school getting to know his people—he therefore "knows" who to approach when (Brigitte O'Malley, Taft Middle School in New Mexico, describing Principal Terry Hannon).

Principal Characteristics

As introduced in Chapter 1 (Figure 1), the characteristics demonstrated by the principals participating in our study mirror the attributes Peters and Waterman say characterize the leadership of "America's best-run companies." Apparently, leadership is leadership, regardless of where it occurs. The eight Peters and Waterman principles—(1) a bias for action; (2) close to the customer; (3) autonomy and entrepreneurship; (4) productivity through people;

(5) hands-on, value-driven; (6) stick to the knitting; (7) simple form, lean staff; and (8) simultaneous loose-tight properties—were attributes subsequently found, through empirical analysis and coding techniques, in the principals we studied. As the study progressed and, characteristic of qualitative research, the eight characteristics were slightly modified as we analyzed our data. Thus, we noted seven leadership qualities that parallel the Peters and Waterman principles.

1. Flexibility in autonomy and innovation
2. Cohesiveness within the organization
3. Commitment to school mission
4. Recognition of staff
5. Problem solving through collaboration
6. Effective delegation
7. Focus on teaching and learning.

To compare our principal attributes with the Peters and Waterman leader characteristics, see Figure 2. "Focus on teaching and learning" was a quality common to *every* principal participating in our study; the remaining six attributes prevailed among the individuals in that group.

1. Flexibility in Autonomy and Innovation

The quality of remaining flexible encompasses three of the Peters and Waterman principles. First, excellent principals are flexible in the "loose-tight control" they exercise over their staff and schools. Second, they encourage "autonomy and entrepreneurship"; yet at the same time, they measure each new proposal against predetermined school goals, reserving the right to give or withhold final approval. Virtually every principal in our study exhibits a "tolerance of failure" by insisting on constant improvement and innovation. Both trial and error are accepted and expected. Third, the best principals are "initiators" who "act now," thus demonstrating a "bias for action" (Hall et al, 1984).

The nature of the organization of schools themselves may be one reason principals who are effective must be adaptable and flexible. Recent research rejects a hierarchical model of classroom bureaucracy as a way to describe schools. The bureaucratic or authoritarian model has well-defined roles, specialization, predictability, a high degree of coordination, regularity, rules and agree-

FIGURE 2.
**Relating Principles of Leadership
to Principal Characteristics.**

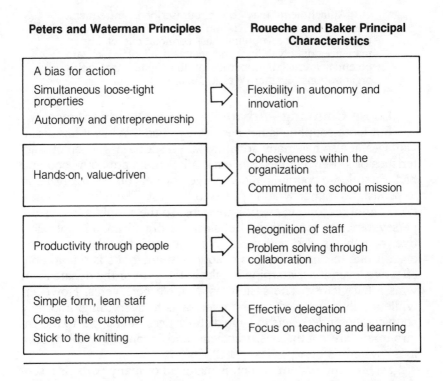

Peters and Waterman Principles

**Roueche and Baker Principal
Characteristics**

Peters and Waterman Principles	Roueche and Baker Principal Characteristics
A bias for action Simultaneous loose-tight properties Autonomy and entrepreneurship	Flexibility in autonomy and innovation
Hands-on, value-driven	Cohesiveness within the organization Commitment to school mission
Productivity through people	Recognition of staff Problem solving through collaboration
Simple form, lean staff Close to the customer Stick to the knitting	Effective delegation Focus on teaching and learning

ment on what the rules are, a system of inspection to see if compliance occurs (accountability), and feedback designed to improve compliance. In this model, there is an emphasis on authority; the people at the top give orders in some way, and the people at the bottom carry them out. The chain of command is clearly defined and highly functional.

However, schools rarely work that way. Instead, they are what Karl Weick describes in the *Administrative Science Quarterly,* March 1976, as "loosely coupled" systems; that is, "coupled events are responsive *but*...each event also preserves its own identity and some evidence of its physical or logical separateness." Weick suggests a metaphor of building blocks. In many cases, one or more blocks can be added or taken away with relatively little disturbance to individual blocks or to the organization as a whole. Thus a portable classroom can be added, a course may be dropped from the curriculum, a teacher may retire and be replaced by another, and the organization as a whole is not disturbed. In loosely coupled systems,

> [A]ttachment may be circumscribed, infrequent, weak in its mutual effects, unimportant, and/or slow to respond....[Loose coupling has] connotations of impermanence, dissolvability, and tacitness all of which are potentially crucial properties of the "glue" that holds organizations together (Weick, 1976, p. 3).

Loose Coupling—Advantages and Disadvantages

But loose coupling is not necessarily "bad." While it has disadvantages, it also has many advantages. Weick names seven characteristics of loosely coupled systems. All of them are both good and bad. First, loose coupling allows some portions of the organization to persist, no matter what happens to the rest. The whole organization cannot respond to every little thing, so the coupling fosters the perseverance of good things. But since the organization is not selective, bad things also persevere. We can see how school goes on, even if one teacher's room is chaotic and another's is remarkably effective, even if a waterpipe breaks in the gym or the debate team wins a big victory. The system as a whole perseveres. However, while a tightly coupled system overreacts to everything, a loosely coupled one underreacts to large disturbances. If changes in the environment are continuous, transient, and inconsequential, then a loose system is best (Weick, 1982).

Second, the system, which is made up of many parts, is a sensitive mechanism. Thus each part "knows" its environment well and can respond to it. Small problems can be sensed quickly and thus solved before they escalate into big ones. But this sensitivity may also mean the system is vulnerable to "fads"; and if a small problem does become a big one, it becomes a crisis because the organization as a whole is slow to respond.

Third, school systems not only sense changes but can adapt to them locally. This is one of the big advantages of being loosely coupled. Because a school, a department, or a teacher can adapt to specific situations, that part of the system can meet local needs without requiring compliance from the rest of the system. But local adaptation can be bad, if the standard behavior of the system is good. If, for example, an overly sympathetic teacher lowers standards for a group of low-ability students, her behavior adapts to the local needs of her classroom as she perceives them; it doesn't affect the other classes in the school, but it is not a helpful adaptation.

A problem with local adaptation is that the environment changes unpredictably. The organization must adapt to current demands, but it must also retain resources for new situations. "Much tinkering looks wasteful because it occurs in the 'wrong' environment. If the present environment changed, some of that tinkering could be 'just what we need,'" Weick says (1982). For example, a teacher "plays around" with computers for years. Then the district decides to buy microcomputers and train teachers in computer literacy. Suddenly, the "playing around" becomes "expertise." However, the organization can't prepare for everything, so the administrator must constantly balance on a tightrope, trying to preserve both stability and flexibility at the same time.

A fourth characteristic of the loosely-coupled system is that it can handle "mutations" without disturbing the whole system. The chaotic classroom, the teacher with low expectations, the principal with poor organizational skills do not affect the other classrooms or other schools. At the same time, a "mutation" that is good can't spread either. In fact, many effective schools are considered "mavericks" within their districts.

Fifth, a breakdown in one part of the system doesn't affect the other parts. But neither can the system easily affect or fix the breakdown. Let's look at an example of a literal breakdown. If a water pipe breaks in the gym, the chemistry and government classes aren't affected. But neither can those students simply be absorbed by the system into other classes for a few days. They may have to wait around, without instruction, until the mess is cleaned up and the pipe fixed.

A sixth quality of the loosely coupled system is that it allows for considerable self-determination. This is both a major advantage and a major drawback to loose coupling. Because teachers in the classroom can determine what will happen there, they feel a great degree of personal efficacy. They have the autonomy to make things happen and can be very effective. These teachers may not have much support from the system, but they don't have much interference either.

The same idea applies to principals in their schools. An effective principal can use weak linkages with the central office to develop a somewhat autonomous and very effective school that is the "maverick" of the system. Of course, the reverse is also true. A high degree of self-determination allows a teacher or a principal to lower standards or permit behaviors that are unacceptable in the rest of the system. Also, people with autonomy are usually reluctant to give it up, so they may be highly resistant to change from outside, as E. Farrar, B. Neufeld, and M.B. Miles point out in their study in the June 1984 *Phi Delta Kappan.*

A final drawback to autonomy is that each autonomous unit has to negotiate its own arrangements with other parts of the system or with outside forces. For example, each department or each school may have to negotiate some of its budgetary concerns. Each teacher has to deal with a parent separately.

Finally, loosely-coupled systems have a low degree of coordination and are thus relatively inexpensive. But because the system is not highly coordinated, it is hard to use for a specific purpose. Each part more or less goes its own way. So if a major change is needed or desired for the whole system, it is hard to design and diffuse throughout the system (Weick, 1982).

Schools—A Combination of Loose and Tight

Let us look at some further implications of loose coupling for schools. Most researchers, including Weick himself, agree that schools are loosely *and* tightly-coupled. The degree of coupling is based on the activity of the variables that two systems share (Weick, 1976). Most schools are looser in matters related to instructional activities and tighter in managerial matters and some matters of pupil control and extracurricular activities, say W.J. Martin and D.J. Willower (1981). The problem is to determine the degree of coupling appropriate for a given situation (Lipham, 1981).

Some aspects of schools are, and must be, tightly coupled. For example, schedules are tightly coupled. Buses must be in the right place at the right time; students are scheduled for the gym, the library, the cafeteria, or Mr. Jones' classroom, and individual teachers or students cannot make autonomous decisions about where they want to be when. Each decision about the schedule has an impact on other people, sometimes many other people, so the schedule is a tightly coupled part of the school. Open classrooms are another example; every action by one person or group affects the other components of the organization (members of the class). People in tightly coupled systems cannot make autonomous decisions without regard for others.

However, instructional matters are usually loosely coupled. One reason is that few participants are specialists, especially at the high school level. The principal has a wide span of control, so "teachers are largely independent of the principal's immediate supervision" (Purkey and Smith, 1982). There is limited inspection and evaluation, and thus little feedback on performance. "As a result, poor performance persists because inattention is justified as respect for professional autonomy," Weick says (1976, p. 673).

It may be that the degree to which the principal "tightens" the couplings, especially in instructional matters, determines the school's effectiveness. As one group of researchers says, "loosely coupled" describes *what is;* "school effectiveness" describes *what can be;* and the most important way to reconcile loose coupling and school effectiveness is by "tightening couplings through school-level policies and enforcement practices" (Murphy et al., 1980). Much of this discussion will describe ways in which principals try to loosen couplings here and tighten couplings there.

Looser at the Secondary Level

Loose coupling is accentuated at the high school level by a variety of factors. One is sheer size. Most high schools have much larger faculties and student bodies than elementary schools, and they are spread out over a wider area, so there is geographical separation. From the principal's view, there is more external coordination, more people.

Second, secondary teachers are specialists in their fields. They work in departments. As a result, they may not even know their colleagues. The effect of one teacher on another is not easily perceived, and teachers tend to be individuated rather than following a norm of collaboration (Blumberg and Greenfield, 1980). As specialists, they feel allegiance to their subject areas; they teach content, not basic skills, so it is hard for them to reach consensus on schoolwide goals and to feel concerned about the school as an organization. The principal doesn't have the expertise to judge personally the quality of instruction, so accountability is difficult, studies say. While coordination among departments may not often be necessary, the necessary coordination is harder to achieve (Farrar et al, 1984).

Finally, loose coupling is accentuated because students move from class to class. Thus, teachers can't get to know all their students well because they have so many for a relatively short period of time. And the movement is an opportunity for disorder and truancy (Farrar et al., 1984).

Being Effective in a Loosely Coupled System

Administrators who take into account the loosely-coupled nature of schools are more likely to be successful. As Weick says, any single policy may sputter; so principals need more effort, more time, more projects, more variety of projects, more talk about direction, and more allowance for individual members to make their accommodations to the idea. Leadership, although considerable in a loosely coupled system, is often diffuse and unfocused. The principal moves the parts of the organization in a common direction. This is more common when the "administrator articulates a direction with eloquence, persistence, and detail" (Weick, 1982, p. 675). The articulation of a common direction serves as a major means of tightening the loose links of a school and is behavior that nearly every effective principal exhibits.

In our study we found that effective principals use certain control mechanisms for coping with the loosely-linked nature of schools. Furthermore, the extent of administrative control varies with each situation. The principals welcome new ideas and encourage innovation, yet at the same time exercise a reasonable control over new policies and programs to ensure their legitimacy within the bounds of school and district goals. Examples offered by staff and by the principals themselves in effective schools reveal that the amount of control exercised by the administration is guided by purpose. Principals of effective schools let overriding principles, such as belief in high standards and administrative support of quality instruction, determine the extent to which they regulate the activities of the staff. For instance, this tendency to take direction, when guiding others, from overall aims and goals is evident in these comments:

> My philosophy of being a "servant-leader" certainly lends itself to having a very unified teacher staff— which encourages autonomy and individual innovation— and, at the same time, to giving me the privilege to maintain control. It's the same philosophy of "when you give, you receive" (Ernest Medcalfe, Warren Central High School, Indiana).

> I see my role not as maintaining control but of being able to facilitate those ideas and practices that we all feel are important. If teachers feel that the administration cares about what they do and will actively assist them in achieving worthwhile aims, the atmosphere established becomes collegial, not coercive, and "discipline" is self-imposed (Alfred Del Herman, Louis Armstrong Middle School, New York).

In addition, many principals of effective schools invite open dialogue without fear of retaliation. C. William Dudley, principal of Wasatch Middle School in Utah, expresses this concern: "A person must provide opportunity to question without threat or intimidation." The theme of autonomy and innovation within the bounds of reason is also echoed in comments made by teachers about their principals:

> Teachers and students know that he is open to their suggestions and more than open to complaints. But they also know that there is a bottom line. Once he makes a decision, that is the end of the matter. These decisions are accepted because we have participated (Carol Lovato, about George J. Bello, principal of Albuquerque High School, New Mexico).

> Dr. Fowler allows me great latitude in using my creativity and innovation as a teacher and still maintains his position as supreme authority in the school. I believe that his ability to do this is inherent in his personality and is evident in the image he projects. I enjoy a sense of freedom in the classroom, but realize that he is at the helm and that there are guidelines within which I must function. He exemplifies the well-known Casals quote: "Freedom, but with order" (Harold D. Peterson, about Delbert Fowler, principal of Highland High School, Utah).

In summary, by exercising appropriate control and by remaining flexible in the management of change and innovation, excellent principals cope with the loose-tight, especially the loose, properties typified in secondary schools.

2. Cohesiveness Within the Organization

Central to well-run companies, according to Peters and Waterman, is "hands-on, value-driven" action. Values are communicated and shared. Likewise, extraordinary principals promote cohesiveness within schools by providing support and understanding to the staff, by maintaining an open door, and by remaining visible around the school in a supportive rather than a supervisory role. Many seek to establish a family atmosphere. Others encourage open dialogue and frequent communication but in a more businesslike manner. While expressed differently among individual principals, concern for cohesiveness within the organization ranks high among their aims and purposes. Cultivating cohesiveness among the staff is another means by which principals of model schools cope with the loosely-coupled aspect of secondary school.

The following examples illustrate some methods used by principals of effective schools to promote a sense of well-being, pride, and unity among the staff. Jenne Lee Twiford of Douglas Middle

School in Wyoming says of Wayne Porter: "He makes me feel that I have the most important job in the world." The ability to influence ordinary people to become excellent is what Angie Mitchell, teacher at Westchester Middle School in Indiana, says Don Deller is capable of doing:

> Taken individually, very few teachers on this faculty could be called outstanding. Most of us are adequate on a good day. Yet Dr. Deller somehow inspires us to aspire to greater things. He has taken us to the top of the mountain, but we have all enjoyed the view.

Another teacher at the same school, Victoria Brock, describes Deller as "never too busy to listen to one of his staff members or students." She adds, "Dignity, pride, respect, and caring are benchmarks of our school."

Teachers recognize the powerful influence principals have in bringing about cohesiveness among the staff. The following excerpts show the extent to which the actions of a good principal provide the catalyst for bringing about togetherness in a loosely coupled organization:

> Mr. Barra mingles with the teachers during nonteaching moments and appears to enjoy our company as people as well as teachers. Many of us consider him to be our friend. He is a calm, flexible, humorous, empathetic, and thoroughly positive individual who loves to be teased. His unflappable good nature has caused the school to be cheerful as well. The four years in which he has been principal of our school have been the very best teaching years for me. I am proud to work under him (Anne Leepansen, teacher, describing James Barra, principal of Valdez High School, Alaska).

> Mr. Young has developed a positive staff morale that is very conducive to the development of strong teaching skills. The staff is made to feel like a team, and each of us strives to uphold the excellence that the "team" is working toward. Working in a "can do" environment produces incredible energy towards the accomplishment of excellence in education. When students and staff believe in themselves, excellence is a by-product of that belief (Linda Rottman, teacher, describing Dan Young, principal of John Rhodes Junior High School, Arizona).

> Mr. Theil makes faculty members feel that they are the reason for our school's success....Interest and concern for a faculty member's life both in and out of the school building is a genuine attribute of Mr. Theil. The ability to boost your ego, or put a smile back on your face,

automatically improves your desire to be a better teacher (Dorothy M. Cord, teacher, describing Robert L. Theil, principal of Clay Junior High School, Indiana).

Principals Describing Themselves

Not only do the teachers' descriptions of principals in our study show that principals of effective schools give special attention to building a unified organization, but the principals' descriptions of themselves illustrate this same tendency. The following comments illustrate how different principals in different schools describe their own actions in attempting to make a loosely coupled organization more tightly coupled:

> An important factor to creating cohesiveness in a staff is communication of the message that each staff member shares in important responsibilities, is accorded professional respect, and is seriously valued as a team member. A "We succeed, I succeed" attitude is valued and fostered by the staff. This is evidenced by 15 organizations within the school raising the funds to cover the expenses of one of our science teachers to accompany his student to the International Science Fair (Sandra McCalla, principal of Captain Shreve High School, Louisiana).

> Administrators do not depart the building until all persons with business to discuss have been met. Frequent stops are made in teachers' rooms, not to observe, but to chat or compliment. Informal pot luck luncheons are held throughout the year to maintain unity among the faculty. Important decisions concerning the school are shared with the faculty and faculty-elected representatives to ensure that they are part of the decision-making processes (Richard Reese, principal of Leesville High School, Louisiana).

3. Commitment to School Mission

A strong commitment to a common purpose and common goals is also related to the "value-driven" Peters and Waterman principle. Excellent principals communicate a powerful commitment to the overall school mission through modelling exemplary behavior and conveying a vision of what the school should and will be. The importance of this personal vision of the school as a whole is a recurring theme in previous studies of effective principals.

Likewise, the principal's personal vision is a strong, recurring motif in the descriptive data relating to principals in our study. The vision most prevalent among our principals involves a strong commitment to the common purpose of a quality education for every student in their daily interactions with staff, students, parents, and the community. With this type of unwavering commitment, principals who direct outstanding schools bring stability to a school. The words of JoAnn Krueger, principal of Manzano High School in New Mexico, indicate the presence of this quality:

> I feel a principal must make explicit what the mission of the school is. Then, every decision and behavior must be consistent with what you say the mission is...and consistent over time and across populations (in other words, students, staff, and parents). The principal's vision is best communicated through directness, fairness, and even-handedness—to the greatest degree possible.

A Sense of Vision

Schools as organizations (not teachers as individuals) seem to be unsure of themselves, to have no sense of direction, no goals. It is hard to promote change, if the organization isn't sure of its essential purpose (Blumberg and Greenfield, 1980). As indicated in Krueger's statement, principals, with their visions, provide this sense of direction. The vision may vary according to the situation and the idiosyncrasies of the principal, but it is present and clear. The school appears focused in direction and moving to achieve a clear purpose.

Schools have many goals for many clienteles, according to William A. Firestone and Robert E. Herriott (1982). The basic goal of schools is fundamental academic competence, but parents and teachers expect more for "excellence." They have such goals as a love of learning, critical thinking and problem-solving abilities, curiosity, aesthetic appreciation, and interpersonal skills (Sergiovanni, 1984).

At the high school level, there is an even broader variety of goals, so that measuring student achievements suggests an "artificially narrow view of the mission of high schools," say Eleanor Farrar and colleagues (1984). High schools must redefine "effectiveness" to go beyond basic skills mastery and define goals that are appropriate for all students (Firestone and Herriott, 1982; Farrar et al, 1984).

"Many or most public schools currently operate with vague, abstract, or assumed goals," the *Research Action Brief* of February 1984 claims. If the goals are multiple and/or conflicting, nothing happens. A school needs a central core of clear, common goals.

Thomas Sergiovanni (1984) believes this vision, this sense of mission and commitment, is what makes a school excellent instead of satisfactory. He believes that three kinds of skills are necessary for competence:

- Technical skills focus on management and routine
- Human skills focus on interpersonal relationships, including participatory management
- Educational skills focus on instructional leadership, curriculum design, and so forth.

All of these are necessary for competence. If one is deficient, then the school loses "critical mass," and less effective schooling occurs. But these three factors indicate competence, not excellence. Excellence exceeds satisfaction. And excellence requires what others call vision and what Sergiovanni calls symbolic and cultural forces. Symbolic forces focus the attention of others on matters important to the school. Cultural forces make the school unique.

Therefore, considerable agreement exists among authorities on leadership that a leader's compelling vision is an essential ingredient for achieving excellence in an organization. Leaders who lack a sense of purpose may achieve competence but will fail to achieve excellence. The principal who defines, strengthens, and articulates purposes, beliefs, and values becomes a cultural leader capable of inspiring the best in everyone. Evident in the comments of Jacqueline McGee, principal of Stephen F. Austin High School in Texas, are the elements of a school culture:

> I proposed a school motto "Everybody is Somebody at Austin High School" which has received enthusiastic endorsement from students, teachers, and parents. A copy of the motto has been placed in every office and classroom. I placed a poster in my office that reads, "My greatest contribution to mankind is to see that each student can learn and grow and feel like a real human being."

At Leesville High School in Louisiana, Principal Richard Reese, has provided an "Excellence in Education" lapel pin to all employees to be worn at Open House, Homecoming, and other public school functions to celebrate the selection of their school as outstanding by the U.S. Office of Education. A gesture like this helps to build a sense of culture and pride in a school. Still other examples of culture-building can be found in written school philosophies like the following:

> Our philosophy is a living document which we review and revise annually. For example, decisions that

affect use of instructional time are made in terms of our stated philosophy (Sandra McCalla, principal, Captain Shreve High School, Louisiana).

A. Lorri Manasse cites Deab and Celeote's concept of "symbolic leaders" who use "myths" to give schools special status and mission. They provide rituals so that diverse outlooks are negotiated into shared ones (Manasse, 1984). A. Blumberg and W. Greenfield (1980) also support the concept of competence versus excellence. They say it seems to be true that most people can learn the attitudes and skills to enable a group of people to function adequately. But not just anyone can lead an organization—a school—in the direction of making itself better than it is. Those who lead effective schools, we have found in our study, are generally charismatic and embody the symbols and traditions that convey a school's culture. Anna Hicks, teacher at Irmo High School in South Carolina, describes the principal, Mr. McCarty, in terms that depict a symbolic leader who communicates the school saga: "Mr. McCarty is a storyteller, a modern-day Will Rogers. For important points he has to make, he has a story to tell." Likewise, Frances M. Racine describes Joseph P. Delaney, principal of Spartanburg High School, in a similar manner: "My principal is a 'Harry Truman' type figure. The buck stops at his desk!"

Dissemination

Effective principals disseminate their vision. They get out of the office and spend time one-on-one. They help people apply the vision, remind them of the vision, help them "interpret what they are doing in a common language" (Weick, 1982, p. 676). In the process they may also seen new ways of defining the vision, which they can then use in further articulation. By helping people tie their everyday activities to the vision, principals tighten the loose bonds between autonomous teachers and the central core.

Creating an Image

But what do effective principals do? They create images of their schools as they would like them to be. Then, using their understanding of the community and the organizational setting, along with their awareness of their own abilities and liabilities and of the resources and strategies available to them, effective principals structure their work, set priorities, and adapt their leadership style to make their visions of their schools into reality (Manasse, 1984, p. 15).

In our study, visibility of the principal and "open-door" policy are behaviors exercised by effective leaders. They engage in and value open, honest, and frequent communication with the staff. They recognize the importance of remaining accessible whenever possible and being visible around the school and at school functions. These examples represent a few of the many we found among principals of well-run schools:

> Dr. Fowler does not stay in his office. He is out in the halls, in classes, and attending activities after school and in the evenings. He knows what is going on—how students react and how teachers function (Hugh Rush, teacher, describing Delbert Fowler, principal of Highland High School, Utah).

> Jerry's door is always open. He always has time to talk to us. He comes to school early and leaves late. He communicates his feelings concerning our performance and suggests alternatives (Tom Shield, teacher, describing Gerald R. Menke, principal of Kearney Junior High School, Nebraska).

> Dale's door is always open, and he's visible in the school. At one point last spring, he heard I was having some particularly rough days. One morning he appeared in my classroom door, called me over, and asked me privately, "What can I do to make your job easier?" (Mark A. Shoup, teacher, describing Dale E. Graham, principal of Carmel High School, Indiana).

Leadership Implies Change

The underlying concept of the vision is the assumption that leadership implies change. The school must move toward the vision, not just maintain the status quo. So effective principals need two types of vision, one of the school and their own role in it, and one of the change process itself, which serves as a framework for daily actions and assessment (Manasse, 1982, 1984).

Change is usually a slow, incremental, long-term process made up of many little decisions and actions (Purkey and Smith, 1982). "Day to day firefighting by itself is unlikely to result in lasting improvements in organizational performance" (Yukl, 1982, p.9). But effective principals use those little things—details, quick decisions—to determine what example epitomizes the vision. They promote the good and ignore the bad, thus helping others see what the vision means and how to help (or hinder) it (Weick, 1982). Manasse uses Vaill's term of "purposing," which is:

> that continuous stream of actions by an organization's for-

mal leadership that has the effect of inducing clarity, consensus, and commitment regarding the organization's
basic purposes (Manasse, 1984, p. 44).

Manasse goes on to describe the purposing behavior of effective
principals. First, of course, they must have a personal vision. Second, they develop an agenda of actions to implement the vision.
They manage the goalsetting process to generate commitment and
vision from all parts of the school community. They have expert
information-sensing skills and analytical abilities and use them to
develop the agenda and to monitor and provide feedback. And they
are skilled in the timely use of conflict management and problem
solving, as dictated by the information-sensing activities. Kay
Swedberg, English teacher, praises the conflict management skills
of George Bello, principal of Albuquerque High School: "If a problem occurs during school hours, Mr. Bello attempts to bring in all
the involved parties at one time for a face-to-face discussion. He is
an excellent mediator."

One of the many parallels between effective principals and
effective teachers is a strong academic posture that combines "few
goals and many methods." The goals are "strongly focused and
clearly defined, but multiple strategies are encouraged, and
teaching staff have the autonomy and flexibility they need to
discover and implement adaptive practices" (Mackenzie, 1983). If
all do not agree on fundamental values (such as hard work or indi-
vidualism), then their goals and behaviors will be different. So principals must help everyone to reach a consensus about values and
goals (Lipham, 1981). They work to clarify and modify goals. And
they model. They are fairminded and hardworking. They expect
teachers to give of their time, so are also willing to give of their time.
Effective principals are concerned and informed; they attend
meetings and inservice training. This deep commitment to their
vision is apparent in these descriptions:

> Casual conversation with Dr. Bates betrays a love of
> (and commitment to) education. She frequently cites
> recent research relevant to the field of education and
> publicly defends educators as professionals (Larry Marrs,
> teacher, describing Sara Jane Bates, principal of Oklea
> Middle School, Oregon).

> Ms. White requires of each person in the building a
> commitment to plan, review, and expand every activity.
> By her example, Ms. White works more than double time
> to provide each staff member with an organized, well-
> considered and comprehensive school plan....Ms. White

always demands that I look at the larger picture. She provides me with many growth opportunities and experiences—introductions to professionals in my field, introductions to community and school resources, opportunities to write three proposals this year, and several opportunities to represent the school to media and school system officials. She always encourages me to explore many professional avenues that contribute to making me a better teacher (Patrick Pope, teacher, describing Ms. Vera White, principal of Jefferson Junior High School Washington, D.C.).

Setting Priorities

Finally, effective principals use their vision as a means of setting priorities so that the instructional program receives the focus. These principals are not consumed by management, although routines are completed. They visibly support the school's improvement program, and they direct the entire program of the school toward their goals. They make management decisions that promote learning. They manage such variables as staff, scheduling, observations, inservice, extracurricular activities, time, class size and composition, organization, and curriculum, with instructional focus in mind. In fact, Manasse concludes that "to some extent, then, the distinction between management and instructional leadership may be artificial" (1982, p. 14). Effective principals manage for instructional priorities. They move the school forward, while freeing themselves for high priorities.

Exceptional principals influence the overall instructional program and the specific learning objectives of students and staff, keeping their vision always before them and integrating as many of their activities as possible toward their goals (Manasse, 1982).

Essentially all principals participating in our study exhibit skill in both management ability and instructional leadership. This quote illustrates this powerful combination of capabilities:

> Our school has increased its enrollment tremendously in the past few years. Mr. Motz has spearheaded a drive for a six million dollar enlargement to our school. Before the plans were finalized, every teacher had the opportunity to speak to the architects about our needs and desires for the new addition.
>
> Mr. Motz was concerned that his staff was not 100 percent computer literate, so he arranged for all of us to take a computer course with a one credit reward toward re-certification. Since that time a new teacher joined the staff and did not know how to use computers in the classroom, so Mr. Motz sent home one of our school com-

> puters to her residence for the entire summer with the
> hope that she would be ready to help the students use
> the computer in the classroom next fall.
>
> Mr. Motz tries to keep up with new theories of learn-
> ing, such as cognitive-matching and left-right brain
> theories of learning, so he also arranged for us to take a
> course on this. He also goes over material in meetings and
> copies pertinent materials for us to read (Marky Maughn,
> teacher, describing Art Motz, principal of Soldotna Junior
> High School, Alaska).

As many writers have pointed out, schools are *both* loosely and tightly coupled. Administrative articulation is not necessary in tightly coupled systems because everyone always shares information. Tightly coupled systems are tied by common goals, appraisals, communication, and interdependent specialists (Weick, 1982). Loosely coupled systems are characterized by autonomy, entrepreneurship, experimentation and growth; so they need leadership that is strong and focused, directed toward creating commitment to a common purpose.

Centralizing with the Mission

The principals participating in our study demonstrate and communicate a strong commitment to a common purpose—in other words, a school mission—in their interactions with staff, students, and parents. These examples illustrate how they "centralize a system on key values":

> Our purpose and mission are evident in Mr. Nesbit's
> genuine concern for the individual student. He knows and
> really cares about our students. If a crisis has occurred in
> the student's life, he is one of the first to visit the family.
> The total school program operates as a reflection of this
> educator's genuine concern. The professional manner in
> which faculty meetings are conducted leaves no doubts in
> our minds concerning our purpose and mission (Connie S.
> Miller, teacher, describing W. Ben Nesbit, principal of
> Spring Valley High School, South Carolina).
>
> We often use the expression "Is it good for kids?"
> Team leaders attempt to keep teams on task in terms of
> improvement, for the kids' sake (Wayne Porter, principal,
> Douglas Middle School, Wyoming).

But administrators can do things besides centralizing on key values. For example, they can centralize the entire organization for a brief period (as in a workshop or retreat). Then the members can make their own accommodation to the values with a more common frame of reference (Weick, 1982).

Many of the principals in our study describe events designed to unify the staff around shared values. At Raceland Jr. High School in Louisiana, Elmo E. Broussard holds breakfast meetings attended by all employees. The breakfasts proved to be so effective that the idea was used for the annual organizational meeting to plan the Raceland Jr. High School Waterfowl and Arts Festival. Others, such as Jo Ann Krueger, principal of Manzano High School in New Mexico, hold staff-wide inservice twice a year sponsored by the district on school time; she has used this time for small group-focused discussions in talking over "how to exchange academic excellence without relying totally on 'punitive grading' and 'motivational techniques.'" Furthermore, Krueger establishes a "School Improvement Team" of volunteer teachers who plan how to improve components of the school which they identify as needing improvement. This group meets in "retreats" at least once a year (with district funding) in addition to their meetings before or after school.

One of the reasons simultaneous loose-tight coupling works is that teachers are willing to recognize, accept, and follow the direction (Shoemaker and Fraser, 1981). They are aware of the organization's norms and expectations, which limit "autonomous" behaviors, but they maintain the autonomy to realize and honor the common core in their own way (Martin and Willower, 1981).

On the one hand, they need to find their lives meaningful, purposeful, sensible; and the common core, the articulated vision of the tight coupling, provides such meaning. But they also need to have reasonable control over their own lives and work, and the autonomy of loose coupling provides such self-control (Sergiovanni, 1984).

The principals in our study give a tremendous amount of support to autonomy and innovation among staff within the framework of school policy. They enthusiastically promote creativity and development of worthwhile, new ideas among their teachers. They allow room for growth, tolerate failures, and maintain a firm yet reasonable control. Successful principals trust their teachers' professionalism and expertise. The following selection lends support to the concept of reasonable control coupled with a freedom to experiment as a means of achieving good results:

> Mr. Williams has always encouraged my trying any new ways I feel necessary to provide motivation for learning and to teach each student as his or her needs dictate. When I felt that we had students who were reading consistently below level and were being lost in the system, he encouraged me to explore the Vocational English program, which brought these students back into a produc-

tive learning environment.

As a result, we have reduced our dropout rate by 75 percent and have increased the chances of these students' being productive members of society. He also encouraged me to initiate a new grading system for these classes. He listened to my rationale and gave me free rein to implement it. This kind of encouragement propels us all on to new efforts (Cheryl Otis Nicola, teacher, describing Bryan James Dinkins, principal of Hazen Public High School North Dakota).

Much of the central vision is articulated through symbol management. "The view of principals as symbolic leaders in loosely coupled organizations is not inconsistent with studies of effective schools and descriptive studies of principal behavior," Manasse says (1982, p. 14). Because of the diversity of strategies and the autonomy of organization members, the principal uses symbols and images to make the vision clear. Symbols, as Weick describes them, explain what and why, while goals are means, telling when and how. Symbols are the large, overreaching explanation of "what's going on here." Goals explain how to get there. They are more adapted to the situation; they are tailored to individuals and/or the local situation (Weick, 1982). While symbols may seem too broad to be helpful, it is precisely because they *are* broad enough to work for everyone, that they are helpful.

Likewise, the principals in our study exercise the use of symbols. Conspicuous posting of the school banner, plaques, pictures, and other items related to school spirit and achievements is common practice among the exemplary schools we studied. In this excerpt, Don Deller, principal of Westchester Middle School in Indiana, describes several ways he evokes school spirit and rallies support around a common theme in his school:

> I believe it is important to establish themes and build motivational components for students and faculty into the school's program. Slogans and special expressions can also capture the spirit. When possible, it is good to use music as well. These are ways to have everyone focusing on common objectives for the school.
>
> Our overall theme since becoming a middle school has been, "Living, Growing, and Working Together...Day by Day." I have taken two songs, sung by the 5th Dimension, to represent this theme musically and play them regularly to stimulate or recapture the feeling of common purpose.
>
> Another is "Friendship Month." During the month of February, we take the opportunity to make every day a special Valentine's Day. Personalized felt hearts are sold

and worn by all students and employees as a way of saying, "I care for you."

These many nonacademic activities, projects, and programs establish the positive school climate that carries into the classrooms. When this occurs, teachers can accomplish with the students their pursuit of excellence.

Finally, Weick summarizes the loose/tight properties of schools.

> The ties in a loosely coupled system are tenuous, which means that the chief responsibility of an administrator in such a system is to reaffirm and solidify those ties that exist. This can be done by a combination of symbol management, selective centralization, consistent articulation of a common vision, interpretation of diverse actions in terms of common themes, and by the provision of a common language in terms of which people can explain their own actions in a meaningful way (1982, p. 676).

Successful principals, then, are leaders with a vision of what their school should look like and be like. They work to build a school culture and to give the school a distinct identity. Through their actions, they communicate unfaltering dedication to the school and to the people in it.

4. Recognition of Staff

Just as Peters and Waterman found that "productivity through people" is key to organizational excellence, effective principals show in a variety of ways that they value the people teaching and working in their schools and recognize their importance in achieving the school's overall purpose. Excellent principals often communicate respect and appreciation to faculty and support staff for their part in achieving school goals. For instance, staff and student accomplishments are frequently recognized and rewarded in high-achieving, well-run schools.

Rewarding teachers is a behavior we found prevalent among the actions of our principals. Dan E. Young, principal of John J. Rhodes Junior High in Arizona, cites some examples:

> The administrative staff shows appreciation of teachers by means of individual recognition through a variety of ways:
>
> — Singling out achievement at a faculty meeting
> — Personal notes
> — "Doin' Good" card

— "Super Teach Award"
— "Super Person Award"
— V.I.P. certificate

We cannot be too generous in recognizing and praising achievement. It must be done often and be deserved.

Sandra Key, a teacher at Jonesboro High School in Arkansas, describes Rodger Callahan:

Our principal's forte is providing positive verbal and written comments about his appreciation of our efforts. Within the past year, for example, I have received a note indicating his appreciation of my attendance of extracurricular activities, a breakfast for not missing any work days during the school year, and a bumper sticker stating, "JHS is Number One because of Me."

On the other hand, principals put pressure on those teachers who do not meet the desired norms. They use the authority of their position to persuade, manipulate, or even force changes on teachers who don't meet minimal standards (Achilles and Keedy, 1983-84; Benjamin, 1981). Ultimately they may try to replace or transfer teachers. At Stephen F. Austin High School in Texas, Jacquelyn McGee faces unsatisfactory performance by teachers honestly and openly by conducting conferences with teachers perceived as ineffective and by developing improvement plans for these teachers. Morris H. (Skip) Pixley, of Sacajawea Junior High School in Washington, maintains quality instruction for students:

We go into the classrooms and make honest observations that over the years have built a level of trust with the staff. We have fired a teacher with 29 years of experience, yet maintained the understanding and loyalty of the staff because the level of trust was so high.

Effective principals do try to maintain a low turnover, but they care more about academics than human relations and don't mind being unpopular if necessary (Benjamin, 1981). So teachers see the principal rewarding conformity to the desired norms and punishing nonconformity to the school goals and expectations.

Finally, in regard to students, the descriptions offered by teachers and principals in our study reflect deep care and concern for students. In the exemplary schools we examined, student achievement is rewarded and recognized. A concerted effort by principals and staff in support of students is articulated throughout the information we have gathered on outstanding schools. Comments by Jerry Menke, principal of Kearney Junior High School in

Nebraska, reveal a sincere concern for faculty and students alike: "Put downs are not accepted in KJHS. We have growth groups for teachers and students. We want everyone to feel important." This sentiment is typical among schools that foster an environment where students grow and achieve.

5. Problem Solving Through Collaboration

This fifth general quality relates, as does staff recognition, to the Peters and Waterman principle of "productivity through people." Problem solving through collaboration requires a willingness by the principal to communicate honestly and openly with people for the purpose of arriving at viable solutions. The best principals acknowledge and use input from their staff to solve critical problems. Additionally, they recognize that solutions vary depending on the situation and that staff members are valuable resources in seeking appropriate answers for meeting demands and resolving conflicts that arise throughout the year.

In a loosely coupled system, teachers have considerable autonomy within their classrooms, and they like it (Tye and Tye, 1984). But as a result of this autonomy, they often have few links with outside sources of information, including their fellow teachers and their principal, and many teachers feel impotent to affect decisions outside their classrooms. This isolation and autonomy should be replaced with a collaborative work effort, so that teachers feel a "sense of family" working together for common goals (Snyder, 1984). The more effective schools talk, plan together, work to improve, and try out new ideas. Rather than maintaining "carefully preserved autonomy," they see teaching as open for scrutiny and discussion (Little, 1982). Success depends on a vision of what is possible, collective reflection and action, and the ability of those involved to work together productively (Snyder, 1984).

Effective principals recognize that goal consensus is important. They pay attention to goal diversity versus uniformity and seek a clear vision that teachers can support. "When the goals of the school are clear, reasonably uniform, and perceived as important, and when the staff is committed to them, successful schools result," J.A. Lipham states in *Effective Principal, Effective School* (1981). Effective leaders are optimistic; they believe constructive change is possible. The fuel for this belief is the leader's value base—what he or she believes is important and is willing to fight for (Cawelti, 1984).

Teachers and principals alike in our study reflect a common belief in goal consensus and cooperative effort yet at the same time have an awareness of differences among faculty. At Katahdin High School in Maine, Loren Ritchie, like most principals who lead excellent schools, "reaches agreement on a course of action" through discussion with his staff: "Goal setting is done through input from departments, committees, and full faculty." These principals of effective schools are actively involved in staff meetings at all levels. The principal of Westchester Middle School in Iowa, Don K. Deller, describes his method of working through people on his staff, as follows:

> I believe it is essential to establish standing committees to deal with all aspects of the school. Further, such committees should be structured to involve people across departmental lines. This breaks down traditional tendencies for teachers to become isolated and possessive. When everyone has a stake in the operations and has a global perspective (like that of the principal), there is greater potential for everyone understanding and appreciating teaching-learning processes and other problems experienced in the various departments.

Departmental, committee, and task force work are common means by which principals of outstanding schools achieve excellence and initiate change. Stacey Savage-Brooks, art teacher at the Louis Armstrong Middle School in New York, tells how her principal recognizes differences among staff, yet provides unity in direction and purpose:

> Mr. Herman's willingness to recognize the diverse talents of the people of the staff makes it possible for faculty members to come forward to offer expertise in specific areas of educational problem solving. Tasks are kept simple and understandable by allowing individuals to use their own personal style to develop effective plans for implementing school programs. When we meet in groups, various solutions are then assessed with the administration giving us goals to meet rather than procedures to follow. Through a participatory management style we all are part of the decision-making process.

In schools where students and teachers perceive a consensus, outcomes are usually high, Squires, Huitt, and Segars say in *Effective Schools and Classrooms* (1979). Consensus builds as groups behave in consistent patterns. Sometimes the consensus is explicitly agreed—when to eat lunch, when to go home. Consensus may hinder the academic process if, for example, teachers give no homework on weekends. A consensus for academic emphasis requires that teachers plan together and that new teachers be taught the consensus (or norms), such as the policies on homework or punctuality. A schoolwide consensus is often a "working" model that can be reviewed and modified (Squires et al, 1979). Obviously, in order to reach a consensus, the principals must involve the staff in decision making.

Effective principals seek advice from teachers, get participation early in the decision-making process, and hold regular and frequent staff meetings (Leithwood and Montgomery, 1982). They involve teachers in important decisions, model open communication, and have an "open door" policy. They frequently meet with teachers, in both large and small groups (Gorton and McIntyre, 1978). They plan ahead by bouncing ideas off of others and are able to accept negative feedback and learn from their mistakes (Center on Evaluation, Development, and Research, 1984). They are active in facilitating communication with the community. Parents are more likely to support the school goals if they are involved in the decision-making process.

Some principals feel that "participatory decision making already permeates all aspects of cultural life" and will become more universal (Snyder, 1984). These leaders don't give orders but facilitate collaboration, informality, and "colleagueship" (Nystrand, 1981). This behavior is particularly appropriate when the staff believes teachers are professionals who have their own expertise.

C.H. Persell and P.W. Cookson, Jr., say the effective principal is open to suggestions and willing to consider alternatives, but this openness is balanced with decisiveness and firm control of the situation (1982). Lipham notes that "successful schools have principals who are strong leaders" (1981, p. 10). The staff is involved in decision making, but the principals accept final responsibility for most major decisions.

Effective principals define the limits of others' participation, so they don't give the impression that others have the power to make decisions when they don't. Getting relevant information and input from others makes the decision more potent. Keith A. Leithwood and Deborah J. Montgomery note that all effective principals have some mechanism for staff participation but safeguard against "serious deflection of the principal's priorities" (1982, p. 326). Mackenzie says the effective principal involves others in the actualization if not the formulation, but must make final decisions personally (1983).

R.B. Greenblatt, B.S. Cooper, and R. Muth list "Ten Commandments of Good Consultation" (1984, pp. 57-59). They agree that effective principals consult first but then make the final decisions themselves. They add some timely pointers. One is that principals should consult only when necessary. As Lipham says, people grow tired of decision making. Group participation is necessary at the beginning; but in the implementation stage, people are ready to act.

Another point is that principals should consult only with staff who have expertise or possess pertinent information—"a deliberate, controlled and limited form of seeking advice, information, and ideas from just those people *involved* and *expert* will work" (Greenblatt et al, 1984). Principals should be certain that staff members are aware that consultation has occurred. Word spreads, and a major purpose of consultation is to establish an open climate, so people know that the principal is modeling consultative behavior. And principals should be sure their information is accurate. As the writers say, teachers don't lie; but all have their own views, so talking with several people tends to give principals a broader perspective. Whether to use an authoritarian, consultative, or democratic style is, as always, contingent on the situation. The appropriate style may vary as the situation develops from one stage to another.

Collaborating in work efforts and planning together exists in virtually every exemplary school in our study. Teacher participation in the decision-making process and open communication are highly valued among the principals and staffs of these schools:

> Mr. Menke *listens* and will change policies if he hears a good idea. He will ask teachers to brainstorm and then isn't afraid to implement teachers' ideas (Tom Shield, teacher, describing Gerald R. Menke, principal of Kearney Jr. High School, Nebraska).

> Each person knows he/she is important because we [the administrative staff members] value his or her suggestions and criticism as the basis for improvement. I encourage input from everyone to improve our program and never take any idea lightly. Faculty and staff can then see the results of their commitment (Joseph D. Delaney, principal of Spartanburg High School, South Carolina).

Using "Team Leadership"

A frequent point from research literature is that the leadership functions do not have to be carried out by the principal alone. *Who* provides the services and certain aspects of leadership is not as important as the fact that *someone* does (De Bevoise, 1984). "Since no one person possesses all of the essential leadership skills, a management team approach seems to be particularly promising for using to advantage the skills of others in the schools," Lipham says (1981, p. 10). The "others" may include assistant principals, supervisors, department heads, curriculum specialists, teachers, and/or other resource personnel. "Team leadership" is especially likely at the secondary level, where there are more administrative units and organizational subunits, and where specialized knowledge is often necessary.

Even when the team approach to leadership is used, principals must do some of it. They have some rights and powers that others do not and can obstruct or support the process of reform enough to make it go or not (Mackenzie, 1983). They are the ones who call in the experts, share the information, and take the initiative. Assistant principals do not usually jump to take the initiative when the principal is passive (Hall et al., 1984). So once again principals are the key—they are the ones, ultimately, who tie everything together in the organizational vision (Manasse, 1984).

Again, in our study, the principals overwhelmingly choose the team approach to decision making, planning, and implementing change. For example:

> Mr. Menke allows us to remain individuals and encourages us to work as a team. He is flexible and willing to examine new ideas and technology. He is not afraid to examine the unknown (Tom Shield, on Gerald R. Menke, principal, Kearney Jr. High School, Nebraska).

> Shared governance gives the faculty a meaningful involvement, and this gives them a desire to work simply and understandably toward the goals of the school (Dorothy M. Cord, teacher, on Robert L. Theil, principal, Clay Jr. High School, Indiana).

> We have built our program over the years through committee work and an effective meeting procedure. They have (as a faculty) realized the many benefits and advantages of regular meetings and good communications among all teachers and administrators. They have accepted the fact there are two reasons for attending a meeting: (1) "What do I have to offer my fellow colleagues?" and (2) "What can I gain by attending?" The emphasis is on giving (Don K. Deller, principal, Westchester Middle School, Indiana).

> Willing participation in open communication is the key in encouraging change and innovation. We plan ahead yet make mistakes and are willing to be criticized for our errors. This cooperative spirit encourages innovation because we are all willing participants in trial-and-error activities (Joseph D. Delaney, principal, Spartanburg High School, South Carolina).

Therefore, curriculum decisions that originate in departments and go up are more popular than top-down models (Gorton and McIntyre, 1978). Changes and later maintenance don't happen without the support and commitment of teachers, who must "buy into" the innovation. Generally, change strategy is "one that promotes collaborative planning, collegial work, and a school atmosphere conducive to experimentation and evaluation (Purkey and Smith, 1982). The principals allow for considerable teacher input, especially for major change. They consult, are open to modification, and recognize the need for teachers to make the change a part of their own lives (Yukl, 1982).

So while typical principals tend to discourage change and facilitate only those innovations brought in from outside, effective principals encourage staff-initiated change. They provide support, commitment, resources, and enthusiastic participation. They initiate changes themselves, consulting with their staffs as they go. And they follow through to see that the innovation is implemented, evaluated, and modified over time.

It is evident that principals of excellent schools also provide support, commitment, resources, and enthusiastic participation to the change process:

> He seeks out articles in professional magazines that he feels I may have a particular interest in. He supports my team teacher and me in new and creative ideas. He allows us to go to workshops with the latest ideas and research in the language arts areas. He makes me feel that I have the most important job in the world (Jenne Lee Twilford, describing Wayne Porter, principal of Douglas Middle School, New York).

> We have pioneered, through the efforts of the staff, many innovative programs that have been adopted by the district. Teachers are continually encouraged to be leaders in the classroom and to be creative in their approach to teaching (Morris H. "Skip" Pixley, principal of Sacajawea Jr. High School, Washington).

6. Effective Delegation

Clear task definition and effective delegation describe a sixth general quality represented in the actions of our effective principals and reflective of the Peters and Waterman characteristic of "keeping the form simple and the staff lean." Exemplary school leaders have the ability to match individual strengths with the tasks where those strengths are put to best use. They not only have a keen sense of which staff members to involve, but also how many it will take to get a job done or a problem solved. Most involve a minimum number of people in order to preserve teacher time for preparation, delivery, and followup of instruction.

These school leaders use common sense techniques explaining assigned tasks clearly and simply. For example, they often break tasks down into incremental planning stages with examples and models provided to guide decisions and actions. Frequently, they will indicate how each task fits into the overall project of school organization, while carefully and specifically communicating outcome expectations. Quite often, faculty and support staff are consulted when deciding exactly what has to be done in order to achieve certain ends. When making task assignments, the principals in our study make personal contact or meet with staff members in a group to review and discuss procedures and, by so doing, gain support and cooperation. Followup on assignments is another important method they use to ensure that the job gets done. However, most are quick to point out that they give autonomy to task groups and keep their own supervision to a minimum. Furthermore, these principals communicate effectively through established and structured lines of communication. When memos are used, they are short, to the point, and few in number. Essentially, involving the right people at the right time is a key skill used by the principals we observed.

Loretta Collier of Booker T. Washington Senior High School in Oklahoma offers this description of the methods she uses to keep tasks simple and understandable:

> I try to ensure that tasks are understood by eliminating communication obstacles at various levels, maintaining an open door policy, and monitoring progress and understanding.
>
> Assistant principals' responsibilities are written as task descriptions rather than as a general job description. Each Monday, during administrative meetings, tasks for the week/month are discussed and clarified in terms of steps needed for successful completion of each task.
>
> Heads of departments convey information to teachers within his/her department and clarify tasks to be completed.
>
> General staff meetings are reserved for information that affects the total staff and explanations are provided. If tasks to be completed are complex, written data is provided, also. If there is a task that can be accomplished

readily with limited involvement, I will sometimes use the services of one staff member.

The principal of Captain Shreve High School in Louisiana, Sandra McCalla, discusses how clear task organization leads to favorable outcomes for students:

> Tasks are broken down into components in incremental planning stages and assigned to appropriate personnel. All responsible parties have knowledge of how their part fits the whole. For example, in designing a coordinated advanced mathematics/calculus program, I defined the problem of students taking sequential courses concurrently and presented the problem to the two classroom teachers. They designed their courses to complement rather than conflict with each other. This allowed our students to complete five college prep mathematics courses in four years.

Also, a clear explanation of expected outcomes is essential to achieving successful results, as illustrated in the comments made by Karen Higgins, teacher at Oaklea Middle School in Oregon, about her principal, Sara Jane Bates:

> Timelines are set up to help simplify complex tasks. She gives the staff guidance and works with individuals or committees having problems. She often sets down parameters so we know the givens and what she can live with.

In sum, making tasks simple and easy to understand and involving the right people are ways that effective principals preserve simplicity yet meet the demands and solve problems in excellent schools.

7. Focus On Teaching and Learning

Every one of the principals in our study expresses "concern for the student" as the reason for the school's existence. Literally all principals involved in our study believe the primary focus of their job is to support and promote quality teaching and learning in their school. In this respect, effective principals ensure that their schools stay "close to the customer" and "stick to the knitting"—the final two Peters and Waterman principles. Working to keep academic activities primary, and keep cocurricular and other activities secondary, is one way effective principals keep schools close to the business of educating. Many of these excellent school leaders have increased students' academic learning time by launching school-wide programs to ensure the achievement of this goal. Although not a surprising conclusion and even though all of the qualities together describe excellent administering, this characteristic of administrative leadership is the most important of the seven cited in our research.

A focus on teaching and learning may appear obvious to most; however, average principals do not focus their administrative efforts unanimously on this area. A typical principal is largely administrative. But an effective principal acts as an instructional leader (Leithwood and Montgomery, 1982). Instructional leadership can and should be encouraged throughout the entire school community, but the principal's leadership is critical. It is one of the rare axioms that almost everyone involved with schools seems to agree upon (Benjamin, 1981). Principals are the keys; they provide consistent, continuous leadership, set the tone, articulate the purpose, build commitment, and guide evaluation (Manasse, 1982). Therefore, a critical distinguishing factor between effective and typical principals is their relationship with the instructional program.

School Climate

In this discussion of instructional leadership, we begin with a synopsis of the contributions an effective principal makes toward a school climate that is conducive to learning and achieving. "Student success is clearly related to school climate, which is, in turn, related to leadership," (Squires et al., 1979, p. 6). If principals have a personal vision of what the school can be, and if they articulate it clearly and then act to move the school in the direction of that vision, they are establishing climate. Much of the literature emphasizes the importance of a positive climate, often using terms of similar meaning such as expectations, norms, tone, culture, and "academic press."

"Norms are expressed behaviors which school personnel find valuable to conform and comply with," according to Achilles and Keedy (1983-84, p. 60). Norms are not policies or rules, although the setting and enforcement of such policies can contribute to norms. Rather, norms are attitudes, standards of acceptable behavior. In effective schools, everyone has high expectations (Little, 1982). Principals believe that they can lead, that teachers can teach, and that all students can learn. Teachers also have these high expectations, and these expectations are transmitted to students. All of these people believe that hard, efficient work improves learning.

These expectations contribute to "academic press," which is "the degree to which environmental forces press for student achievement on a schoolwide basis" (Murphy et al., 1982). But academic press is broader than staff expectations. It includes school policies, practices, norms, rewards, standards—everything that makes up the school environment. In effective schools, teachers take responsibility for all students all the time, so students in the halls between classes are held to the same standards of behavior as students in classrooms (*Research Action Brief,* 1984). In an orderly climate, students aren't testing the limits all the time; instead, they know what the limits are, and they stay within them. Discipline is firm, fair, consistent, and quickly enforced.

Our information about the behaviors that characterize princi-pals of exemplary schools includes a wealth of excellent examples. The policies, practices, norms, rewards, and standards reflect com-ponents which, when taken together, compose an orderly school environment:

> Teachers know that the number one objective is to ensure that students learn. However, attitude and learn-ing climate have the greatest effect on whether students learn. I devote the majority of my energy to establishing a positive school climate. . . a place where students want to come. . . because "something great is going to happen to me today and I don't want to miss it," and a place where teachers enjoy coming to work because "it's fun to be with the people in the building."
>
> This climate permits an informal, lateral (rather than vertical—adult to child) relationship that enables the stu-dent to see teachers caring for them as individuals. When students know teachers genuinely care about them, they are more positively receptive to learning, guidance, and other efforts made *with* teachers to pursue excellence. This is accomplished through a daily homeroom and co-curricular activities program, special positive-rallying activities, and special projects in the various instructional areas (Don K. Deller, principal of Westchester Middle School, Indiana).

The concept of climate and that of the symbolic leader are tied together in the term "culture." As mentioned earlier, Sergiovanni (1984) describes both a symbolic leader and a cultural one. Symbol-ic leaders are the "chiefs." They model important goals and behaviors, thus signaling to others what is important. They use "purposing," that continuous stream of actions that communicate the purpose of the school. They articulate their visions, stir commit-ment, and provide others the means to communicate about their behavior in relation to the goals. Cultural leaders are the "high priests" of an organization. They build the legacy. They socialize new members, telling stories, maintaining myths, traditions, and beliefs. They explain "the way things operate around here," and use symbols and rewards to establish the culture, the norms, the consensus on goals.

D.L. Clark and L.S. Lotto (1984) cite Ouchi's view of the school as a clan. The clan has a strong leader and willing followers. The staff chooses to share values and socializes new members to those values. It has a working environment in which all participate and share. It has a safe environment in which participation is ensured over a long period, and its members identify personally with the organization and its activities.

Again, the feeling of shared values and a personal sense of identification with the school is illustrated over and over among the narrative descriptions offered by the teachers and principals participating in our study. Several examples of this cohesiveness are below:

> In an atmosphere permeated by a desire for excellence in teaching and learning, Dr. Deschamps has set no limits. What he has said, in effect, is: "You are intelligent teachers. Now bring those students in your charge to their fullest potential as young adults. Let me know what I can do to smooth your path as you, the teacher, work toward that goal" (Don Ribbing, teacher, describing Dan Deschamps, principal of Parkway West High School, Missouri).

> Mr. Bello is always willing to listen to a problem and to offer help. He can be found in the hall every period of the day, and he wanders in and out of the classrooms. He is very interested in his students and teachers. Frequently when he is in a classroom, he looks over the students' shoulders and asks them questions about the subject (Kay Maureen Swedberg, teacher, describing George Bello, principal of Albuquerque High School, New Mexico).

> We have weekly faculty meetings in which Mr. Ritchie constantly reminds us of the need to "pick up" a student when down and to communicate with parents with positive statements as well as when a student is in trouble. He visits classes and keeps a journal with positive statements for all faculty to see in the teachers' lounge (Chester Chase, teacher and assistant principal, describing Loren Ritchie, principal of Katahdin High School, Maine).

Teachers and others in the school are made to feel important because of the individual attention they receive from the principal. He usually greets teachers in the morning as they come by the office, is available to talk to teachers, praises the teachers individually in faculty meetings and in bulletins....

Although Spring Valley is a very busy school with many activities going on simultaneously, the principal always brings into focus our primary purpose, which is teaching and learning. As the school calendar is planned, school assembly programs are considered, activities are promoted, the principal keeps these important activities from interfering with the teaching and learning aspect of our school....He gives a person a job to do and leaves him alone to do that job and then praises him when the job is done well. He exhibits excitement over innovative challenging and creative ideas which create challenging learning environments for our students. When you do your job, he pats you on the back and encourages you to do more (Sharon Deal, teacher, describing W. Ben Nesbit, principal of Spring Valley High School, South Carolina).

Ability to Change and Innovate

Culture varies considerably from school to school and with the elementary and secondary levels (Firestone and Herriot, 1982). Secondary schools are more complex and diverse so efforts to change the culture are more difficult, but the culture can be manipulated for academic effect (Purkey and Smith, 1982).

According to S.C. Purkey and M.S. Smith, the culture model "assumes that changing schools requires changing people, their behaviors and attitudes as well as school organization and norms. It assumes that consensus among the staff of a school is more powerful than overt control, without ignoring the need for leadership" (1982, p. 68). These kinds of changes—values changes—are slow and incremental (Blumberg and Greenfield, 1980). Innovations and bold initiatives occur rarely; routine, day-to-day interpersonal contact is the way principals change climate (Yukl, 1982). These face-to-face encounters are usually informal; and they often occur in the classrooms, hallways, and other building sites. These encounters provide a symbolic function since they convey a certain image of the school. The principal thus fosters relationships among individuals who are loosely coupled, and the linkage provides a sense of unity (Strother, 1983).

In these descriptions, it is evident that the principals engage in many informal interpersonal encounters day-to-day and that by so doing build positive relationships and a climate right for innovation and change:

In a simple, quiet way, Mr. Johnson lets us know we are appreciated....He repeatedly says indirectly that we do a good job. He can laugh at himself. His door is always open, and he listens (Wesley W. Maiers, teacher, describing Garth Johnson, principal of Valparaiso High School, Indiana).

Phil has a tremendous way of talking to people. He makes you feel very worthwhile and "needed" within the school. He is always dropping in to see what is going on. He is always ready and willing to discuss an idea or problem *right now* instead of next week. Phil always gives positive strokes. He has a gift for getting a lot of mileage from his staff without their even knowing it (Susan Eide, teacher, describing Phil Barra, principal of Valdex High School, Alaska).

One important norm that effective principals try to promote is "risk-taking among staff. Continuous change in programs in the direction of better serving student needs [is] considered highly desirable" (Leithwood and Montgomery, 1982). Teachers are rewarded for initiative, risk-taking, and continuous change. Once more, the principals in our study appear to advocate change and risk-taking:

I work primarily with students who are identified as gifted and students who are monitored for identification. I have been able to implement a mentorship program, revolving-door program, and an after-school interest program for these students. I have built towns in my classroom, held language festivals, and constructed a museum that covered an entire wing of the school.

Mr. Cogar understood the need for all of these activities and gave his support. He has even gone so far as to offer the school as the host site for a regional Olympics of the Mind competition next year. Mr. Cogar respects the teachers, and the teachers respect him. There is a mutual understanding of purpose and of roles (Levi Clayton Folly, teacher, describing Paul N. Cogar, principal of Prospect Heights Middle School, Virginia).

I am often asked to speak at in-school and out-of-school functions which included a conference in Albany, a presentation to Mrs. Louis Armstrong, and various meetings with visitors from other schools. Mr. Herman brings observers to my room often, always noting how special and effective my program is.

Perhaps the greatest vote of confidence was Mr. Herman's asking me to be part of the 6th grade core program as a language arts teacher. Being an art teacher for six years prior, I felt a bit thrown by this switch in

roles. Having taken the time to get to know me, Mr.
Herman quickly and demonstratively reframed this order
and made it a challenge, giving me his complete faith
that I could do it and he knew it! It *indeed* turned out
to be my most rewarding year in teaching.

Mr. Herman definitely has conveyed his trust in me
by being supportive of all of my ideas. He helped me
launch my art portfolio class for 8th graders applying
to specialized high schools by allowing me to offer it as
an elective class. He gave me an art intern to develop a
mini-workshop in museum management, which culmin-
ated in the portfolio show designed and hung by the
students (Stacey Savage-Brooks, teacher, describing
Alfred Del Herman, principal of Louis Armstrong
Middle School, New York).

Modeling Desired Behaviors

In order to foster the desired climate, principals engage in a
number of behaviors. The most obvious is that they model desired
behaviors. Norms are cyclical; that is, what is considered appropriate dictates how members behave. If it is appropriate to believe
that all students can learn, then the behavior of teachers and students reflects this belief. But if the staff believes that students can't
or won't learn, then behavior reflects this belief. Principals demonstrate their beliefs by modeling. For example, if tardies are not
punished, then students will be late consistently. If tardies are
acceptable behavior, the implication is that instructional time has
little value (Squires et al, 1979).

The following selections suggest a few of the behaviors
modeled by our principals:

School and teaching are Mr. Motz' life, and this rubs
off on us all. He is never without an uplifting word and
always is pleasant. There are not worries about where
one stands with him. Teachers at his school are tops
(Marky S. Maughan, teacher, describing Art Motz, principal of Soldotna Jr. High School, Alaska).

George Seagraves is a dedicated, conscientious
educator. His enthusiasm for learning is contagious; he
challenges faculty and students to strive for excellence.
Never too busy to listen to the concerns of others, he has
earned the respect of faculty, staff, and students.

He genuinely cares for young people, and they value
his concern. Students are perceived and treated as responsible young adults; accordingly, they not only live up to
expectations, but also in many cases, exceed them.

A sense of self-discipline and order prevails across
the campus; mutual respect exists between students and

faculty; every teacher is expected to be firm, fair, and friendly with each student. Our classroom climate fosters learning in a nonthreatening environment, and the opportunity to teach is unencumbered (Excerpt from a letter, signed by all department heads, supporting the nomination of George Seagraves, principal of Lee County Senior High School, North Carolina, as outstanding educator and administrator).

Principals model in many ways. They are "on-task." They are active, involved participants in the learning process. An orderly, safe environment is important, so they avoid "institutional neglect." Broken windows are fixed, equipment is kept in good repair, and the building is clean. They get out in the building to observe, discuss, monitor, provide feedback, and generally model. They provide the resources that teachers need, thus obliging teachers (implicitly) to conform to the desired norms (Achilles and Keedy, 1983-84; Strother, 1983). They monitor teacher behaviors such as homework assignments and punctuality and provide feedback by conferring with teachers. They reward students for academic success by giving them responsibilities so that they feel their actions have an impact, and their self-concept improves (Squires et al., 1979). The following selection from our study reveals a conscious effort on the part of the principal to act as an example for his staff:

I attempt to convey a common purpose to all faculty by making all efforts to serve as a model for the teachers. It is an expectation at this school to be punctual, be prepared, pay attention to detail, follow through effectively, and communicate well. The administration attempts to reflect this by observable behavior (Dan E. Young, principal of John J. Rhodes Junior High School, Arizona).

Finally, principals contribute to a climate of high expectations by supporting teachers. Indirectly, this behavior is a form of modeling an emphasis on instruction. A primary means of supporting teachers is with time. Effective principals reduce the number of noninstructional interruptions and tasks so that there is a maximum of instructional time. And they arrange the schedule to provide time for planning and teaming.

Effective principals also serve as buffers for their teachers. They protect teachers from organizational pressures, outside interference, parental protests, and/or too many simúltaneous changes. They act as shock absorbers. They reward teachers who are meeting norms by providing time, resources, pats on the back, public recognition and greater responsibility. "Time on task" is an axiom for the principals we studied. They describe specific schoolwide policies and activities that support increased learning time:

> The teaching-learning act is the most important thing that happens in our school. Each person clearly understands this and works to protect classroom time. All other activities are examined and controlled in light of how they affect the teaching/learning. Our policy is that no student can be absent from a teacher's classroom to participate in an extra activity without the approval of the classroom teacher (Loretta Collier, principal of Booker T. Washington Senior High School, Oklahoma).

Instructional Leadership

In this final section on effective principals, we summarize the research literature on instructional leadership. The section following the summary reviews our findings on instructional leadership from our sample of principals.

Some critics say that principals have little effect on classroom practices. And indeed, if it is true that many principals do not focus on instructional leadership, then it is easy to see why they don't affect classroom instruction (Rutherford et al, 1983).

However, effective principals are instructional leaders. Many of the behaviors an instructional leader exhibits are those we've discussed as being characteristic of effective principals. Instructional leaders are initiators. They look for ways to move the school in the direction of its goals and are not content to leave teachers alone (Leithwood and Montgomery, 1982). They use their discretionary powers to allocate time and resources in ways that support the instructional program. They are willing and able to manipulate the system for their programs, even if they have to "rock the boat." They have a personal vision of what the school can be and articulate it clearly and then act on it so that all members of the organization become tightly coupled around that vision. Instructional leaders establish a climate or culture of high expectations (Morris et al, 1982). They actively model desired norms, including risk-taking and reward those who conform to the norms (Crowson and Porter-Gehrie, 1981). They also spend time out in the building, making the many small decisions that add up to "leadership" and "culture."

Instructional Leadership at the Secondary Level

Leadership is an important quality in all of the effective school research. Most of that research has been done at the elementary, not at the secondary level where teachers have significantly greater influence over day-to-day classroom management decisions (Firestone and Herriott, 1982). However, Hall and his colleagues at The University of Texas at Austin found that, contrary to testimonials about time, management duties, expertise, and so on, many high school principals are effective as instructional leaders and change facilitators. They are in the classrooms, things are happening in their schools, and the principals are identified as the catalysts (1984). Effective principals, unlike typical ones, are actively concerned about several aspects of instruction, including strategies, resources, allocated time, an orientation toward academics, and establishing and maintaining priority instructional behaviors over long periods (Leithwood and Montgomery, 1982).

Increased technology and, at the secondary level, specialization means that principals cannot possibly acquire all the knowledge necessary for personalized, subject specific support of teachers. Instead, principals know the issues and techniques of effective teaching. They identify appropriate expertise and resources, provide incentives, and orchestrate the processes for bringing resources to the staff and putting them to use (Manasse, 1982). Effective principals provide the staff with knowledge and skills, directly or indirectly. They may go into the classroom and/or work one-on-one, but at the secondary level, the direct responsibility for curriculum and supervision may lie with others (Little, 1982).

The typical principal, on the other hand, provides a minimum of support and that may involve only physical arrangements; effective and typical principals are equally concerned with the ready availability of materials and resources within the classroom (Leithwood and Montgomery, 1982). Typical principals provide little if any orientation for new teachers, and they often have poor relations with the central support staff (Leithwood and Montgomery, 1982). A principal in a large urban high school may be involved in instructional leadership only through indirection, or providing climate and vision, not training or direct observation (Morris et al., 1982). However, even teachers involved with highly structured programs say that a principal's backing is necessary if the program is to be successful (Benjamin, 1981).

How do instructional leaders support their programs, especially if they do not provide direct supervision? First, they communicate their high expectations clearly (Rutherford et al., 1983; Murphy et al., 1982). Their goals are focused on student cognitive growth and happiness. Most teachers share those goals, so there is tighter coupling (Leithwood and Montgomery, 1982).

Second, they provide resources, especially time. They facilitate department meetings and hold more meetings for department heads (Pinero, 1982). They provide planning time, protect instructional time, and monitor the effective use of classroom time (Squires et al., 1979; Murphy et al, 1980; Pinero, 1982).

Third, they protect and reward teachers. They shield teachers from threats of public interventions or criticism (Pinero, 1982). They allow teachers to make autonomous decisions within the overall framework of the school goals. They reward cooperative behavior and effective teaching through such means as desired summer school assignments, promotions (if possible), and high ratings on evaluations (Crowson and Porter-Gehrie, 1981). They ensure smooth organizational processes, including the provision of an orderly, safe environment (Pinero, 1982; Sweeney, 1982).

Effective principals get involved in the instructional program of the school. They direct efforts to update and use curriculum guides (Pinero, 1982). They use faculty meetings to discuss student achievement and curriculum (Sweeney, 1982). They have a strong knowledge of instructional practices and are actively involved in planning, if not actually carrying out, instructional programs.

Effective principals communicate the importance of the instructional program to the community. They serve as the linkage in the loose coupling between the school and external factors, including parents and the central office (Miskel, 1977). They share achievement data with students, teachers, and parents and communicate the importance of such data (Sweeney, 1982). Typical principals, on the other hand, establish friendly but non-substantive relations with the community (Leithwood and Montgomery, 1982).

Providing Focus and Feedback

Finally, effective principals help students focus on achievement. They set schoolwide policies on homework, grading, remediation, reporting progress to parents, and retention or promotion (Murphy et al., 1982). They reward student achievement in various ways, including assemblies and exhibitions of student work.

Effective principals monitor both teachers and student and provide feedback. They gather information about teachers, collected openly from classroom observations and conferences (Squires et al., 1979; Leithwood and Montgomery, 1982). This information is used to help teachers, either through direct shared feedback or by providing guidelines for needed inservice programs (Leithwood and Montgomery, 1982). Teachers are more satisfied when the evaluation criteria are known, when they are evaluated frequently, and when the evaluations are reported back to them frequently (Persell and Cookson, 1982). Typical principals, on the other hand, fail to consider teachers' emotions or values. They rarely go into the classroom. When they get information about a teacher, they do not use it or share it (Leithwood and Montgomery, 1982).

Effective principals also monitor the world outside the school. They gather information about new practices, the world of work, and the wider school system, so they can use this information to make decisions about the instructional program.

Instructional leaders also monitor student progress and assess the instructional program. U.C. Pinero (1982) describes several ways that this is done: They use standardized test information to examine progress. They use criterion-referenced tests to see if students are achieving school goals and objectives. They examine and discuss grade reports with teachers. They use student achievement data to discuss progress and programs in faculty meetings and with individual teachers. And they provide feedback to parents and community members.

As we have indicated, supervision of teachers may be done directly by the principal, or it may be done by instructional specialists. At any rate, the principal is responsible for its occurrence. In loosely coupled systems, there is little need for coordination between teachers or for very close supervision (compared to a business manager, for example). In fact, teachers prefer the autonomy inherent in loose coupling (Yukl, 1982). As a result, according to Mackenzie (1983, p. 12), "the effective principal is less likely to prescribe specific methods than to offer continual assistance in response to the problems which teachers identify for themselves." Mackenzie cites Tomlinson's point that school effectiveness comes down to behavior changes in the classroom, to effective teaching; so staff development should focus on teaching, learning and classroom decision making, and effective teacher research.

Effective principals try to improve instruction by becoming involved with the recruitment and selection of teachers. While they are constrained by district policies and the negotiated settlements of teacher organizations, they may try to use their discretionary powers to attract or keep good teachers. Many principals want greater autonomy in personnel issues (Lipham, 1981). Once teachers are hired, effective principals try to match them to students, since a "good fit" is likely to increase teaching effectiveness and student achievement (Leithwood and Montgomery, 1982).

Finally, instructional leaders promote change as the school

moves in the direction of its goals. Change does not occur naturally. There are obstacles to overcome, and intervention is necessary (Leithwood and Montgomery, 1982). The principals' support is necessary for successful change (Squires et al., 1979). They provide support in a number of ways. First, they show commitment for the concept at the outset. They work to achieve role clarity for the participants. They buffer the staff against environmental pressures. They secure and provide the necessary resources, and they provide social support and active participation themselves (Squires et al, 1979). Effective principals know the innovation in detail. They know the research and can demonstrate the program or give assistance. If they have only general knowledge, then they provide less visible support, the innovation is "uneven and generally short-lived" (Little, 1982). Effective principals develop trust and serve as sounding boards. Typical principals are more formal or authoritarian. They don't comment one way or the other, so their support is weak, at best (Leithwood and Montgomery, 1982).

Our Findings: Instructional Leadership

The foregoing brief summary of the recent research conducted on effective principals as instructional leaders reflects very closely the characteristics we found among the principals in our study. Typical in qualitative analysis, our hypotheses have been developed from our collected data through the process of examining the descriptive information (for example, hypotheses were not formulated beforehand). As with the analysis of teachers, a code book for the principals has been developed, springing from an initial sample of the entire group of principals. Characteristics were extracted from the sample, categorized into groups, and developed into a code book used to score the presence or absence of these characteristics in the entire number of participants. This method was devised from the procedures used by Klemp and Spencer in their study, "Analysis of Leadership and Management Competencies of Commissioned and Noncommissioned Naval Officers in the Pacific and Atlantic Fleet" (1977), in which code books were also developed, using the same process. Independent of our code book development, we conducted a search of the literature pertaining to effective principals. Interestingly, the characteristics of effective principals described in the summary of the research parallel almost exactly the qualities exhibited by the principals of exemplary schools represented in our study and outlined in our code book.

For example, every principal in our study demonstrated instructional leadership.

Our principals tend to be charismatic, cultural leaders whose main concern is the quality of the teaching and learning occurring in their schools. These dynamic leaders know what is going on in classrooms, communicate the goals and objectives of the school to the staff and the students, work to acquire a capable faculty, support a cogent curriculum, and seek to provide a conducive school climate. Don Ribbing, Parkway West High School in Missouri, describes the instructional leadership of his principal, Daniel Deschamps:

> Philosophy is not an empty word for him or for the staff. The philosophy of the school hinges on teaching and learning. The awareness of this is renewed directly and indirectly throughout the year. Together we created the philosophy, and we bear witness to it in the way we are. By his words and acts, he creatively inspires us to keep it fresh.

Likewise, at Albuquerque High School in New Mexico, George Bello, principal, is portrayed in comparable terms by James Owens:

> Mr. Bello is very concerned with student learning at AHS. He's not only concerned with the feelings of parents, teachers, and the community toward student learning, but honestly believes that each student must feel that his or her personal education is of the greatest importance.

Furthermore, good principals in their interactions with students express a genuine concern for learning:

> Mr. Young frequently stops students to check on their homework and the books that are being taken home. He also rewards the students as they achieve in grades or attendance at our school with achievement passes—passes that allow students to enter activities free of charge (Margie Eustice about B. Donald Young, principal of Simon Perkins Middle School, Ohio).

The principals in our study frequently visit classrooms both formally and informally. They make a conscious effort to know what transpires in classrooms from day to day. Carol Lovato tells how George Bello at Albuquerque High School keeps up with what is happening in her classroom:

> He will visit classes unannounced for short periods, quietly and without fanfare. One proceeds with one's

teaching as though he were not there. He conveys
approval directly on an individual basis to teachers. He
may commend teachers in writing. He has submitted
names of members of this staff for awards by community
organizations. He knows the value of praise and uses
praise carefully and well.

In addition, many of the principals teach classes themselves
occasionally to help out and to keep "a hand in," so as to understand teachers' problems more readily.

Not surprisingly, the principals who stay in touch with the
classes in their schools expect a great deal from their faculty and
the students. High expectations are the key to high achievement.
Excerpts from a letter written by a former student to Rodger
Callahan, principal, and faculty at Jonesboro High School in Arkansas, reveal the value of expecting the best: "In the last year, I found
that I knew information that I thought was basic, while other new-
comers in college were totally lost during lecture....I have faith in
the high standards that are set at Jonesboro High." Our study
indicates that principals of schools that maintain high standards
clearly communicate these expectations to faculty and students.

Choosing the Right People

Building a strong, capable faculty with diverse talents is
another way these effective principals sustain a focus on teaching
and learning. They begin this critical process by hiring only the best
teachers. "I hire teachers that are interested in kids," says Jerry
Menke, principal of Kearney Junior High School in Nebraska. "I
select strong staff and then place trust in them to make good
decisions," states Jacqueline McGee, principal of Stephen F. Austin
High School in Texas. JoAnn Krueger, principal of Manzano High
School in New Mexico, expresses her awareness of the importance
of choosing the right people: "Selection of new staff, when positions
are open, show where a principal's values and emphasis lie."

In addition to actively recruiting and hiring superior teachers,
the principals in our study supervise and evaluate faculty constructively and provide frequent opportunities for professional
development. Sensitive to the needs of the staff, they support
teachers' attendance at professional meetings and workshops, as
well as provide inservice that fulfills those needs.

Supporting and Developing Curriculum

Furthermore, these principals of exemplary schools demonstrate a focus on teaching and learning by supporting and developing a well-grounded curriculum. In Larry Marrs' opinion, his

principal at Oaklea Middle School in Oregon, Sara Jane Bates, does just that: "She supports educational programs with resources—time and money—and goes to battle to upgrade current curriculum and maintain quality programs." Similarly, Angela Ramirez, a teacher at Taft Middle School in New Mexico, expresses appreciation for the efforts of Terry Hannon:

> One thing that I've been most grateful for from Mr. Hannon is the fact that he always found a way to support my speech program. I take students four times a year to city speech and drama meets. The cost for these meets with entry fees and transportation is excessive. Mr. Hannon has always provided us with a bus and paid our entry fees so that we don't have to raise the money ourselves. No car washes, candy sales, etc! That means more time on task in the classroom. Terrific!

Three leadership behaviors related to curriculum—emphasizing achievement, setting instructional strategies, and coordinating instructional programs—are also demonstrated by the principals in our study:

> A strong academic program has top priority in our school. According to the new educational standards passed by the legislature in Arkansas, we do not have to come up to them; we are already there. This is because Mr. Callahan has foresight in planning our curriculum and keeps abreast of changes taking place in education (Fran Burgess, teacher, describing Rodger Callahan, principal of Jonesboro High School, Arkansas).

Another example of this emphasis on a solid curriculum is illustrated in words to Thomas Drake, principal at Indian Hills High School in Iowa, which clearly indicate where his priorities lie: "A principal cannot only be a cheerleader for a teacher's ideas; he needs to be able to find the time, funds, and resources to assist the teacher in completing the idea."

Therefore, in the exemplary schools we have studied, we find a strong emphasis by the principal on the teaching and learning going on in the institution. The information collected indicates that exemplary schools have dynamic leadership, especially in instruction, provided by the principal. Furthermore, principals of outstanding schools tend to recruit and retain capable faculty, to develop a well-grounded curriculum, to communicate clearly defined school goals, to monitor and reward student and faculty achievement, to seek collaborative effort in problem solving, and to convey a strong commitment to a common purpose—that is, a school mission that centers around quality instruction.

In conclusion, the characteristics of well-run companies tend to match those of high-achieving schools. That is, the principals participating in this study exhibit these seven attributes:

- Appropriate control to allow teachers autonomy within the bounds of school policy
- Cultivation of cohesiveness within the organization
- Strong commitment to a vision of what the school ought to be
- Reward orientation
- Simplicity in task organization and delegation
- Collaborative effort
- A focus on learning and teaching.

These seven leadership characteristics appear to culminate in excellence within the school and the education it delivers.

CHAPTER IV

EXCELLENT TEACHERS

W hat makes a teacher effective? It's a seemingly simple question. We know from our own experiences in school that some teachers are more effective than others. Most of us can remember and even name two or four or even a dozen teachers who stand out as beacons in our classroom experiences. Perhaps we should rephrase the question. Given that there are effective teachers, how do we know when we see one?

The answer is, of course, both arguable and complex. However, recent research provides evidence that effective teachers share certain common characteristics. Of course, not all teachers exhibit them in the same ways, and one teacher may place more emphasis on one characteristic than another, but all effective teachers, no matter the grade or subject or socioeconomic level they teach, seem to share certain characteristics. If we know what the characteristics are, we can recognize an effective teacher.

In our review of the literature, we selected and read only a portion of the hundreds of articles and books written about teachers over the last decade. Some of these articles were written by researchers who observed and/or interviewed teachers in their schools, then analyzed their data and drew conclusions. Other articles were written by scholars who reviewed and summarized research findings. And others were written by educators whose experiences in schools and teacher education programs have made them experts. We need to keep reasonably clear the distinction between field research and logical, but unproven, expert opinion (Ralph and Fennessey, 1983).

There have been more studies of elementary than of high schools, especially elementary schools that are in urban settings, are poor, and have high percentages of minority students (Rutter, 1979; Centra and Potter, 1980). Elementary schools are typically small and focus on the goal of teaching basic skills. The instructional techniques most effective in elementary schools (where basic skills are taught to children) are often not appropriate in secondary schools (where more complex thinking skills are taught to older students).

Studying high schools is more difficult because they are larger and more complex than elementary schools. They are divided into departments, and many teachers are specialists within their departments. It is difficult for a school to focus on one or two specific academic goals that apply to all students in all classes.

In addition, the input variables are more difficult to control—that is, ninth-graders or seniors have a more varied range of skills, knowledge, motivations, and needs than do first- or fifth-graders. And unlike an elementary teacher, a high school teacher has less than an hour a day, sometimes for only one semester, to make a difference in the life of an individual student. High school students are less motivated by a desire to like and to be liked by the teacher. Subconsciously, at least, they understand many of the theories of learning and motivation, and they can both manipulate "the system" and resist manipulation by it (Troisi, 1979).

Most data on schools are correlational, not causal (Purkey and Smith, 1982). That is, we can say that Behavior X correlates positively with Result Y, but we can't say that Behavior X *causes* Result Y (although the correlations are sometimes so consistent that we want to make that assertion). For example, a certain teacher exhibits high expectations for her class, and her students perform well on both behavior and academic measures. Do her high expectations influence their achievement, or does their record of achievement influence her expectations? Who is influencing whose behavior? Obviously, this question is difficult, if not impossible, to answer: researchers respond by saying that high expectations and high achievement have a positive correlation, not that one causes the other.

One way to examine effective teaching is to select a characteristic (or several) and then go into classrooms and look for it: how often does this characteristic occur? Is there a relationship between this characteristic and high achievement (effectiveness)? Another way is to identify effective teachers (using several criteria) and then observe what those teachers do—and don't do. Our study takes the latter approach.

With both approaches, researchers usually have to divide or sort general characteristics, such as "classroom management" or "clarity," into a set of single, observable, measurable behaviors. They observe the frequency of the behaviors, collect data, and analyze it to determine which behaviors, if any, correlate with high achievement. Sometimes the observable, measurable behaviors lose the essence of the original. For example, how do you measure "warmth" or "enthusiasm"? In the final analysis if we think these behaviors are important characteristics of effective teaching, we must be able to explain how the teacher exhibits them and how much is enough.

Despite these caveats, which researchers and experts are quick to mention, *common characteristics of effective teachers* have emerged from both our review of the literature and from our study. The teaching characteristics we have identified in our study are inter-related and are in close agreement with previous research. Both the literature and the results of our study indicate that these behaviors correlate positively with student success and achievement and, taken together, define what we believe to be an effective teacher.

Through empirical analysis and coding techniques, we have found the 12 Selection Research Institute (SRI) teaching themes extensively demonstrated by the excellent teachers in our sample. As the study progressed, we modified the SRI teaching themes as the data were analyzed and produced a list that was then divided into three groupings—defined by Klemp (1977) as characteristic of superior performance among people working in all careers. Klemp's categories—*motivation, interpersonal skills,* and *cognitive skills*—each served as an organizational umbrella for four general teaching themes (for a total of 12). In this chapter we present our findings with an introduction to each category and a discussion of the teaching themes clustered there (See Figure 3.).

Motivation

According to Klemp, cognitive and interpersonal skills alone do not guarantee effective performance; motivation is a critical factor. He defines motivation as "a need state—a prerequisite for be-havior" (Klemp, 1977, p. 107). Consequently, in our study we have

FIGURE 3.
Excellent Teacher Characteristics.

Motivation	Interpersonal Skills	Cognitive Skills
Commitment	Objectivity	Individualized perception
Goal orientation	Active listening	Teaching strategies
Integrated perception	Rapport	Knowledge
Reward orientation	Empathy	Innovation

looked closely at the responses of excellent teachers for clues that might explain what *motivates* good teaching. We also wanted to identify specific cognitive and interpersonal skills possessed by outstanding teachers.

Through our research we identified four factors in the motivation of excellent teachers:

(1) They have a *strong commitment* to their work and to their students. (2) The majority are *goal oriented,* with high expectations for themselves and for their students. (3) Many view the world in a holistic fashion. In other words they have *integrated perception.* This ability to see the big picture, combined with skill in developing strategies for meeting goals, enables these teachers to fit everyday learning activities into a broad learning spectrum. Consequently, they see beyond the specific, daily, classroom interactions to the larger, general purpose of helping students become productive and self-reliant individuals. (4) Finally, and perhaps most important, the single most motivating factor in their day-to-day teaching is their *reward orientation.* When students improve and grow, the dynamics of success are set into motion: students who achieve become hooked on success and attempt to succeed again. From students' successes springs the satisfaction that motivates and powers the drive of excellent teachers.

Strong Commitment

An essential characteristic to superior teaching is commitment. In education, commitment means showing a deep dedication to one's chosen career and valuing the teaching/learning process as a valid way to achieve society's goals. In our study, we define commitment as a belief that students can reach their potential and that a teacher's primary purpose lies in making significant contributions to others.

Positive Expectations. Effective teachers believe that all students can learn and that they as teachers can promote that learning. They see learning difficulties as obstacles that they must overcome, and they search for appropriate techniques that will help each student learn. Instead of presenting material and abandoning students to learn it any way they can, these teachers feel a responsibility to provide both the means and the opportunity for learning.

Studies have shown repeatedly that a teacher's belief in a student can have a profound effect on the student's ability to learn (Ornstein, 1982). Perhaps rather remarkably, the ability to learn appears, at least in part, to be linked to an outside source—in this case, the teacher's belief in the student. It has been demonstrated that students are significantly better able to learn under the tutelage of someone who *assumes* that they can (Good et al, 1975). Susan Eide, Valdez High School in Alaska, shares a viewpoint held by many of the excellent teachers in our study: "I have the philosophy that all students will learn in my class. There are no exceptions to this rule. Some students take a little more effort on my part, but I think the payoff is worth it!"

Whether labeled "high expectation," "academic press," "a climate for expectation," "optimism about the potential of students," or "positive expectations," researchers generally agree that effective teachers believe that all students can and all students will learn and behave appropriately. A teacher's responsibility is to provide the means of success, but there is no doubt in the teacher's mind that success is achievable. As Rutter notes, "[p]eople tend to live up (or down) to what is expected of them," and these expectations apply to behavior as well as academic achievement (Rutter et al., 1979; see also Brophy, 1981; Gage, 1978). The large majority of the teachers in our study expect high level achievement from their students. The words "to the best of their ability" or "to do their best," appear repeatedly throughout teacher responses. For example, Tom Shields, Kearney High School in Nebraska, writes: "I believe everyone should strive to do her best. You get what you expect....I encourage them to shoot for the moon." The teachers represented in our study demonstrate that they know what students can do best and are able to challenge students to develop their potentials fully.

Teachers express these expectations through clear verbal communication. At the beginning of the year, they explicitly describe student behaviors they expect regarding assignments, routines, and objectives. They then regularly enforce deadlines, routines, and other shared requirements. They are friendly but businesslike in attitude. Modeling task orientation, excellent teachers expect students to behave similarly. By increasing allocated and engaged time, they emphasize instructional tasks and project a serious regard for the learning process. Our later discussion of teacher-generated classroom management techniques describes specific strategies for keeping students on task and out of trouble.

Good, Biddle, and Brophy report that teachers pitch their instruction to a "steering group," a group of students used as "benchmarks" to determine comprehension, pacing, and the need for further practice. "In general, the higher the ability and achievement of the steering group in a classroom, the higher the learning shown by the class as a whole. Teachers who aim higher generally produce better results" (Good et al., 1975, p. 61). These high expectations and resulting successes produce positive results for students, including higher self-esteem, a higher self-concept regarding ability, and improved internal locus of control that often transfers to areas outside the classroom. And since these attitudes correlate with success, they may also correlate with achievement, motivation, and behavior.

Teachers who have high expectations of their students assign meaningful homework. Studies have shown that frequent homework is correlated with better behavior and academic achievement. A word of caution about homework—though studies also show that unless homework provides *needed* practice or sparks future interest (by relating to personal goals), it can have a negative influence on student learning. Homework for discipline's sake is punishment. Homework has "symbolic importance" because it places emphasis on academic progress by reflecting the expectation that students can and will work independently, without direct teacher supervision, and reinforces the high academic expectations that the teacher holds for the class (Murphy and others, 1980; Strother, 1984). The teachers in our study strongly support the role of homework in conveying and maintaining high expectations by checking and commenting on daily, in-class and homework assignments.

Furthermore, they develop good study and organizational habits in their students. According to other research literature and our findings, teachers demonstrate their high expectations by modeling, by making demands on students, and by helping them set and achieve goals. They model such behaviors as punctuality, organization, emphasis on academic tasks, and neatness. They demand attention in class, care and accuracy in student work, and makeup work. Each of these small tasks helps students feel their work is important; and as each task is accomplished well, students feel successful.

These teachers not only demand achievement, but they provide opportunities for it (Murphy and others, 1980). They select appropriate materials, teach the material thoroughly, monitor frequently, provide much feedback to each student, reteach if necessary, and are especially careful to ensure student success on new material or individual work. Consider the philosophy of Adelaide De Medeiros, teacher at George V. LeyVa Intermediate School, California:

> I try to encourage each one to capitalize on his own
> strengths and set small goals for improving the weak-

nesses. The student is made to feel good about his strengths and, from them, can draw the strength to deal with an attainable goal in improving his weakness. For example, a student may be doing poorly because of attendance. After pointing out that when he is there, the work he does is good, I then focus on the improvement of attendance as a goal.

Effective teachers make students accountable for their learning (Murphy and others, 1980; Mackenzie, 1983). They teach students how to pace themselves and then expect class assignments to be completed in time (Brophy, 1982).

They also make them responsible for bringing their own materials, for studying, for paying attention, for completing individual and/or independent assignments. They help students establish realistic but challenging goals and find the means to achieve them. And in the process, these teachers make students aware that their performance is the result of their own efforts. Students come to realize that success is not based on some external factor such as "luck," but that they can consciously determine their own success.

Good teachers do not encourage dependency, rather they strive to teach students how to learn for themselves. Barbara Dilley, Soldotna Junior High School in Alaska, conveys the satisfaction she feels:

In our math program, one of the greatest responses is. . . the students who indicate they have taken responsibility for their own learning. When a student tells me that I must hurry to help him because HE needs to get to work, I know that it is not my great and glorious performance that makes the difference, but his need to feel important about his own learning.

More specifically Margie Eustice, Perkins Middle School in Ohio, explains her strategy for making students responsible for their own learning:

Throughout the year I try to increase the responsibility of the student toward the goal. The first six weeks I allow extra credit with written directions and suggestions that I have prepared. As the year progresses more and more responsibility is put on the student to work on his or her own for ideas and direction for extra credit as well as for regular class requirements.

Thus, effective teachers express a strong commitment to teaching through a positive outlook. They expect excellence from students, and they get it. However, they encourage students by helping them to establish and reach demanding, yet realistic, goals. They do not leave the learning process to chance, but purposely sequence learning tasks. Through this process, the students experience repeated successes that affirm their self-worth and cause them to grow both personally and academically. By accentuating students' capabilities, superior teachers help students to mature into their roles as learners and to become independent, curious, questioning individuals.

Commitment to Students Outside of Class. At the college level, Schneider, Klemp, and Kastendiek found that effective teachers are accessible outside of class, and they are available to average as well as to superior students (1981). Roueche found that effective teachers have "a commitment to the profession" (1982). And it seems reasonable to assume that a teacher who is available before and after class or during office hours is more likely to have good rapport with students, see them as individuals, and be perceived as enthusiastic. Rutter and colleagues noted that the number of students who talked to teachers outside class had no direct correlation with academic achievement alone but did have a correlation with successful schools when the four measured outcomes in the study were combined. They also noted that the teacher's willingness to talk outside of class is an example of positive modeling (Rutter et al, 1979).

A different kind of outside commitment is implied by effective teacher behaviors within the classroom. Effective teachers are involved with students during class, so they must use non-class time to plan, prepare activities, and grade papers. Goodlad reported 10 to 15 and sometimes more hours a week spent on preparation for high school teachers. Using data from both elementary and secondary levels, he suggests:

> ...a minimum of 37½ hours of work per week, a modal range of 40-45, and a high of just over 50. Clearly, teachers who seek to plan very carefully, to create alternative kinds of classroom activities, or to assign and read essays regularly cannot do what they expect of themselves within a normal work week (of 35-40 hours) (1984, p. 170).

Many teachers are also involved in cocurricular activities; they sponsor clubs and attend non-class school functions, such as plays, sports events, or PTA meetings, on their own time. However, there is no evidence in the literature that these activities have any bearing on classroom achievement, though we can speculate that they contribute to the teacher's perceived rapport and enthusiasm. Nonetheless, in our study, the great majority of effective teachers indeed demonstrate a strong commitment to students outside the classroom, in addition to their dedication in class. While many of our excellent teachers talk about working for community-school involvement, a larger number keep close contact with parents, especially parents of children needing special encouragement; advise cocurricular activities; and provide additional help to students whenever necessary.

High schools especially have many diverse activities—athletic, musical, social, and academic events—and teacher support is a necessary ingredient in this total educational experience. The effective teachers we studied enthusiastically participate in these cocurricular duties. Charles West, Kearney Junior High School in Kearney, Nebraska, describes his involvement:

> I offer my students the opportunity to grow by volunteering my time in county spelling bees and by coaching volleyball....Giving students avenues of performance gives me great satisfaction.

Anna Hicks, Irmo High School in Columbia, South Carolina, expresses commitment to students' total growth through her appreciation of their interests and activities:

> I love 17 and 18-year-olds. I try to attend their games, dances, and graduations. I have chaperoned the senior trip to the Bahamas three times, and I would never miss the prom!

Thus effective teachers, as indicated in their responses, spend hours outside the normally-scheduled classes in coaching math teams, directing plays, rehearsing bands, supervising the production of school newspapers and yearbooks, training athletic teams—contributing actively to the entire social system.

Not only are the excellent teachers in our study involved in cocurricular activities; they are also available to both remedial and advanced students during time out of class for academic and personal counseling. Often class time is an insufficient instructional period for a student who is deficient or needs extra work, and teachers sacrifice their personal time in order to be accessible to their students who need more guided instruction. Kay Swedburg, Albuquerque High School in New Mexico, says:

> I encourage students to excel every step of the way in every bit of learning. To that end, I ask students to

redo assignments. I also offer help outside class—before
school, during lunch, after school, and on weekends.

Some of the teachers we studied provide other learning experiences.
John Strang, Valdez High School in Alaska, provides some such
opportunities:

I enjoy hunting and fishing and other activities with
the kids. These activities are great in gaining experience for science.

Tom Shield, Kearney Junior High School in Nebraska, again expresses commitment to students extending beyond the classroom:

If the day comes when I don't feel a deep sense of
commitment to the education of children, I will switch
professions. I travel the extra mile many times over in an
effort to ensure that my students are getting all they
have the right to expect from me.

Goal Orientation

People who set personal goals and seek models for themselves
in terms of their personal values are motivated to excel. In our study
the large majority of participating teachers establish personal goals
and determine a course of action for attaining them. A common process involves clarifying personal values and then transferring these
values into manageable goals. "If I am clear about what I value,
then my goals become clear," explains Marjorie Ratliff, teacher at
Lake Oswego High School in Oregon. David Arnold, Clay Junior
High School in Indiana, further explains how goals provide focus in
his personal life and in his teaching:

I am a goal-oriented person. I use a daily checklist
of "things to do," set long-term goals in several different
areas, and modify those goals on a regular basis. As a
teacher, this same system of goal setting is used. Students
are constantly reminded of the high goals I have set for
them. They are encouraged to set their own goals, also.

Some teachers in our study elaborate further on the theme of
goal-orientation by discussing their own role models. For them,
models help in setting high standards in their teaching. Kay Swedburg, Albuquerque High School, discusses her role models:

My model has been those teachers who taught me.
Those who were excellent, who proved caring, who de-
manded the best of me, and who took the time to lead the
way are the ones I have attempted to follow. My father is
a good example. Not only was he a good teacher, but he

encouraged me by saying, "Be the best you can be." He
told me to continue learning so my mind would always
be open. That I have continued to do.

Goal setting and making references to role models are frequent
traits of excellent teachers and appear to correlate positively with
high-achieving students. A clear majority of the teachers in our
study establish goals in their own lives and in their classes, re-
vealing a strong sense of direction both personally and
professionally.

Integrated Perception

A third major teaching theme found among our exceptional
teachers is the quality of viewing their students and their teaching
holistically. We refer to this characteristic as "integrated perception." Students are viewed as whole individuals operating in a
broader context beyond the classroom. This view of students in-
fluences an excellent teacher's approach to teaching, classroom
examples, and methods used to teach concepts.

Nearly half the exceptional teachers surveyed in our study por-
tray this ability to perceive the larger picture. We venture to suggest
that this quality is developmental and will appear primarily among
the teachers who have years of experience. As evidenced in the
teacher responses, "integrated perception" may further identify the
most outstanding teachers among those identified as exceptional.
Math teacher, Harold Piatt, Manzano High School in Albuquerque,
New Mexico, expresses a "big picture" view that has emerged over
his many years of experience with young learners:

> I must keep reminding myself as I prepare lessons
> and plan teaching techniques that I do not teach mathe-
> matics, but rather, I teach students. My goal is to teach
> them to understand mathematical concepts so that each
> student can reach as high a level of understanding as she
> is capable of, so that she can do what she might someday
> wish to do. To accomplish this I must be aware of the
> total student—her abilities, interests, problems and needs.
>
> More important than the mathematics that a student
> learns, is that a student learns *to learn*. The process of
> learning mathematics provides excellent opportunities for
> a student to learn how to read, to organize thoughts, to
> separate hypothesis from the conclusion and to begin to
> develop an understanding of inductive and deductive
> reasoning. It also provides excellent opportunities for a
> student to develop the ability to relate to other people.
> Study time in the classroom is a constant buzz of activity
> and conversation as students converse with students and

> students with the teacher concerning problems and
> solutions.
>
> Seldom does a class period go by that a student does
> not have the opportunity to go to the chalk board, work
> a problem, or illustrate a concept and explain it to the
> class. Without the student being aware of what is going
> on, we will work on poise, organization, and grammar
> along with mathematics. I feel this accomplishes two
> things. First, personality is woven into an otherwise
> abstract subject; and second, the student has an oppor-
> tunity for self-expression.

This awareness of overall learning goals in day-to-day teaching
practices is characteristic of teachers who demonstrate an integrated perception in their approach to teaching. Responses of
exceptional teachers reveal an overarching perspective that provides a framework for daily lessons. Charles Fitzsimmons, Perkins
Middle School in Ohio, conveys such a view:

> Over the years I have determined that my role as a
> science teacher is to teach students how to think and
> solve problems. The subject matter covered in the class-
> room is the vehicle by which this is done. Most students
> are not going to become scientists, but they will need to
> think and solve problems. Activities must lead in some
> way to these goals.

Tresa Taylor Hadnot, Leesville High School in Louisiana, also reveals an integrated perception: "I try to give my students an idea of
the continuity of things. I give them at least one year-long project
and relate specific assignments to it." Three more outstanding
teachers offer a macrocosmic view in everyday teaching. Don
Ribbing, Parkway West High School in Missouri, relates the following example:

> I tell students I expect them to grow and to transfer
> what we have dealt with in the classroom into the living
> they do....I want them to reflect on the literature (I teach)
> and the ideas it spawns. I encourage them to bring these
> topics up at the dinner table so that what happens in the
> class does not happen in a vacuum.

Larry Marrs, Oaklea Middle School in Oregon, says, "I teach to life
itself, rather than to a test." And finally, Stacey Savage-Brooks,
Louis Armstrong Middle School in New York, reflects a world view
expanding beyond the classroom:

> Man is a microcosm of the universe, and I teach my
> students to recognize the rules of nature evident in them-
> selves. In the spring, I asked them to find signs of spring

> in themselves....One of the compositions I got back
> called "The Seed" is a child's realization that his life
> follows a pattern found elsewhere in nature.

Thus, integrated perception among exceptional teachers provides unity and continuity in daily lessons and further develops an understanding of facts and concepts within a larger context. Holistic teaching develops the total individual and helps students link the knowledge gained in the classroom to their lives in the total environment. Through this process, learning becomes meaningful, useful, and relevant for every student.

Reward Orientation

The negative aspects of education are common subjects for discussion today. Frequently cited challenges to a good educational program are: low salaries, long hours of extracurricular activities, lack of respect for school authority, and electronically-pacified or chemically-stimulated students. What then keeps excellent teachers fresh and eager to learn and share knowledge, to participate in personal relationships with students, and to contribute to the meaning of life in general?

One answer: effective teachers get great satisfaction from seeing the learning process "work." They receive not only monetary income from their jobs, but also " 'psychic income'—the enjoyment that comes from seeing a child's face light up when an idea takes hold, when a concept is mastered, when a skill is learned" (Futrell, 1984, p. 12). These teachers are pleased when their students experience success, such as getting into college or getting a job that indicates long-term retention or independence. We speculate that this "psychic income" may be the source of teachers' enthusiasm and high expectations. This enthusiasm is reciprocated by students as they try to meet these expectations. In fact, the overwhelming majority of excellent teachers in our study describe this source as the most important motivating factor in their efforts to be good teachers. Representative comments are:

> The spark that keeps the teacher coming back is seeing the light come into the student's eye. It is the motivation for all else the teacher does (Marcia Mendenhall of Indian Hills Junior High School, Iowa).

> Seeing students learn and achieve is the reason I am in teaching. If it were not for what the students give me back in seeing what they accomplish, I would not be able to stay in teaching (Larry Wood of Wasatch Middle School, Utah).

> I believe what does set me apart from other teachers
> is the fact that I receive extreme satisfaction from my
> students' successes, no matter how minute, and am
> always crowing about these successes to everyone within
> earshot (Anne Leepansen of Valdez High School, Alaska).

These and other responses from excellent teachers clearly indicate the critical importance of "psychic income" in motivating teaching excellence.

The satisfaction a teacher receives from student growth originates with student response rather than with the teacher's own performance. That is, effective teachers are rewarded when students exhibit understanding, achieve their goals, and become independent learners pursuing interests on their own and successfully applying acquired knowledge and skills to real-world situations. The teacher's satisfaction is heightened when students and parents recognize and express appreciation for the teacher's efforts through notes, cards, or just a thoughtful word.

One of the most heartfelt tributes among the responses to our study was written to Maryetta Ferre, Terrace Hills Jr. High School in California, by a former student. The letter is presented here in its entirety as a summation of the warmth and sincere appreciation felt by many who have had the good fortune to learn from an exceptional teacher:

> *Dear Maryetta,*
> *Here we are ready to begin another phase of our friendship. Before we do, I must take this opportunity to share some feelings with you. When you were my seventh grade teacher, you were my inspiration. When we met again years later, you were my model. This seems an inadequate way to express my thanks, but I hope you will accept the gesture.*
> *The year you were my teacher, I decided to be a teacher. Although my father was a teacher, it wasn't until that year that I consciously felt the influence an adult could have over a child. It shaped not only our behavior, but our attitude toward self and others. You called us "ladies and gentlemen." And I hope, for the most part, we acted like ladies and gentlemen. Do you remember when we walked out of homemaking? You didn't assign us detention. You talked to us about respect and human feelings. Do you remember encouraging me to run for class officer a second time, even after a first defeat? I remember. Did you really feel the enthusiasm for the things that you taught that we sensed? I'm not afraid of "bees," I can still read the "stock reports," I understand the "expanding and contracting of matter when cooled and heated," and I still have my report on Greece along with all the paraphernalia. It was stimulating to be in our class!*

At 12 I couldn't label the things that you were doing right. But as I studied teaching, I began to recognize them: You were a master of motivation. You helped us to bridge from what we knew to the outside world. The atmosphere was orderly and structured, and we were supported. We regularly received feedback and sought to find out how we were doing. We felt successful and interested. You gave data. We weren't floundering for facts or suffocated with dittos. We were involved.

When I had a classroom of my own, I wanted it to be just like the one we had experienced. The first time you came to visit, I was so proud that you could see my work.

When you came through the staff development program, you confirmed my belief that good teachers want to be good teachers. Good teachers are dedicated and willing to put in additional time and effort to achieve the quality of excellence they attain. When I visited your room for the "coaching visit," I fully expected to come away with more than I had brought. I did. Your presentation was just as the lesson plan model had prescribed.

I'm confident, beyond a shadow of a doubt, that you will be as inspirational in the new position as you have been previously. I'm so pleased that our paths continue to cross and look forward to the time we have to work together in the future.

Yours very sincerely,
Patty

Although this quality of reward orientation has not received much attention in previous research studies, some have recognized "psychic income" in motivating exceptional teaching. Our study indicates this orientation, the satisfaction received from student achievement, is one of the strongest motivating principles among the teachers we investigated.

It appears, then, that great teaching is inspired by the simple, yet beautiful act of one human being touching another through the learning process. We, consequently, encourage further investigation into greater use of the reward and recognition of exceptional teaching for the purpose of motivating and producing quality instruction.

Summary

We have identified four major factors in our study that appear to motivate the exceptional performance of excellent teachers: a strong commitment, goal orientation, an integrated perception or holistic view, and reward and satisfaction from students' successes. We will turn now to a description of the interpersonal skills we find among extraordinary teachers.

Interpersonal Skills

Effective teachers work to establish a supportive, non-threatening climate in the classroom through:

- Active student involvement
- Feedback—praise and criticism
- Verbal fluency—the ability to rephrase and clarify responses
- Enthusiasm—which the teacher fosters by modeling
- High expectations of student performance.

An effective teacher provides a comfortable, supportive environment in which students are willing to participate and become involved in learning. Brophy and Good, in a study of teacher expectations, note that students, like teachers, are different and respond to teachers in different ways: "Other things being equal, student response to teacher behavior will be reciprocal (teacher warmth and initiation will lead to student warmth and initiation; teacher coldness or hostility will lead to student withdrawal or hostility; and so on)" (Brophy and Good, 1974, p.39). Troisi cites studies which conclude that:

> ...academic studies are not very important in adolescents' lives (as most teachers had surmised)....The student must have a positive, caring perception of the teacher if the teacher is to receive that cooperation which will result in increased student achievement (1979, p. 7).

In other words, the positive climate may not be a direct cause of learning, but it does provide an environment in which students are likely to take advantage of learning opportunities.

How do teachers establish this comfortable, supportive climate? They model desired behaviors. For example, they are willing to express their own feelings; they can articulate shared experiences. They are willing to make mistakes and thus demonstrate that it's okay to fail sometimes.

Effective teachers find out " 'where students are coming from;' i.e., how their situation affects behavior or orientation" (Schneider et al, 1981, p. 56). They learn students' names quickly and make a specific effort to learn about student interests, often in the first or second class meeting. They then attempt to match course content with the interests, experiences, and goals of the class.

These teachers indicate concern and interest in students' lives but are careful not to cross the line between active interest and embarrassment, intimidation, or harrassment (Guskey and Easton, 1983). They make a point of encouraging effort and praising the average as well as the superior student, providing caring support so that students are willing to become involved. If corrective feedback is necessary, these teachers focus on the behavior, not the person, thus displaying an "objective" approach to discipline.

In one interesting study, Barbara Ware asked high school students to choose the rewards or recognition they valued most (from a list of 15, compiled by other students). School programs usually focus on extrinsic awards, such as plaques, trophies, certificates, or public name recognition. However, the students' top four choices were more intrinsic than extrinsic and thus "probably the hardest for a teacher or school system to implement" (Ware, 1978, p. 356). These four choices were:

- Reaching a personal goal
- Receiving a scholarship for school
- Getting compliments and encouragement from friends
- Being accepted as a person and having others seek their opinion.

When asked how teachers might help them achieve these valuable rewards, students replied that teachers should:

- Teach goal setting
- Give moral support
- Listen
- Teach students how to give and receive compliments
- Encourage sharing of successes
- Teach communication skills
- Recognize individuals as important and worthwhile.

Students like teachers who foster a comfortable climate. A survey of 566 Little Rock students, grades 7-12, produced a popular response; students liked a "positive relaxed learning environment" with a teacher who "jokes and makes learning fun, talks on the level of the students...expects that all the students will learn, (and) is patient and understanding" (Mosley and Smith, 1982, p. 273). However, Good, Biddle and Brophy cite a number of studies at the secondary and college levels which indicate that "teacher behavior involved in maximizing student learning is not always the same kind of teacher behavior involved in maximizing student attitudes"

(Good et al, 1975, p. 78). In other words, the teacher who is rated highly by students is not *necessarily* the one from whom students learn the most. As one group of researchers put it: "Satisfying human relationships is a necessary but insufficient condition for student learning" (Murphy and others, 1980, p. 68). Rosenshine summarizes:

> Effective formal classrooms are not cold and critical....Teachers in formal classrooms today are warm, concerned, flexible, and allow much more freedom of movement. But they are also task-oriented and determined that children learn (1979, p. 50).

The excellent teachers investigated in our study contribute to a positive, supportive learning climate largely through effective interpersonal skills. Our study identifies four major skills or competencies in this relationship-oriented category: *objectivity, active listening, rapport,* and *empathy*. Around each of these four factors clusters an array of teacher behaviors that contribute to a nonthreatening, classroom atmosphere conducive to meaningful learning.

Objectivity

Appropriate discipline techniques help maintain a supportive, task-oriented, classroom atmosphere. Teaching routines are carefully patterned to *prevent* disruption, so that energy can be directed toward learning-related activities. Effective teachers do not permit disturbance to begin; they have a variety of "preventive maintenance" behaviors. In fact, studies show that once the cycle of disruption begins, effective teachers are no better than the ineffective in dealing with it (Brophy, 1982; Good and others, 1975). The difference is that effective teachers keep trouble at bay in the first place, a conclusion supported in our findings. Participating teachers report numerous, positive, preventive methods of maintaining orderly classrooms. Consequently, disruptions occur infrequently; and when they do begin, these teachers approach the problems objectively and methodically. Connie Miller, Spring Valley High School in South Carolina, demonstrates:

> In my classroom teaching, I feel my understanding of teenage behavior and the forces behind their behavior allows me to be objective. I accept my students as individuals with varying needs and diverse backgrounds. I have no need to demonstrate power and control. I respect my students and expect them to respect me. I take a personal interest in each student, and they know I care.

I express my concern for them before any classroom problems can develop.

Effective teachers have "withitness"; that is, they are aware of what is going on in the classroom. This is a form of monitoring. These teachers frequently "scan" the entire classroom so that they can spot both academic problems and incipient disruptions.

"Withitness" leads to "overlappingness," the ability to do more than one thing at a time. "Overlappingness" may occur when, for example, the unexpected happens, when several kinds of activities are going on at once, or when students are working individually: a teacher working with one group may speak to a student who is off-task in another while noticing that a third group is finished with its task.

Effective teachers reduce or eliminate disruption using one or more of the following techniques:

- "Signal interference"—using eye contact or hand gestures
- "Proximity control"—touching or standing near the student in a relaxed manner. If the teacher is moving around the room anyway, this technique does not cause further disruption
- "Tension release"—using humor to reduce tension in the classroom
- "Lesson restructuring"—changing the plan when it isn't working. Teachers may stop and reteach a point before students continue practice, or they may provide additional practice beyond the original plan, or they may stop one activity and go on to another in order to replan and/or restructure the unsuccessful activity for the next day
- "Support from routine"—setting patterns of behavior. For example, if a student has lost her pencil, she can ask several neighbors if she can borrow one, or she can follow an established routine, such as borrowing one from the teacher's "pencil box"
- Removing "seductive materials" such as athletic equipment, magazines, radios, or hats that distract the attention of one or more students from the learning task
- "Antiseptic removal"—sending a disruptive student on an errand, to get a drink of water, or otherwise removing the student from the scene of the disruption (Ornstein and Levine, 1981, p. 594).

If a disruptive situation does occur, effective teachers keep in mind their dual purpose of fostering learning and reducing time off-task. In this regard, they try to keep the problem from affecting other students, so the teachers' interference is quiet and often individualized (Rutter et al, 1979). Because of their "withitness," these teachers target a "guilty" student correctly (Billups and Rauth, 1984). They also keep self-control, realizing that "roughness"—anger and frustration on a teacher's part—produces student anger and further frustration (Coker et al, 1980; Ornstein and Levine, 1981). They enforce rules and routines quickly, providing corrective feedback to stop bad behavior and thus modeling enforcement for other students. They have a fair, preestablished hierarchy of consequences, so that "the punishment fits the crime" and all students are treated equitably. Effective teachers try to handle disruptions themselves, in the classroom, knowing that a student who is removed from class is not learning. However, they remain task-oriented and in control and are not willing to let one individual disrupt the learning of the whole class for long.

Sheri Childs, Captain Shreve High School in Louisiana, illustrates several of these techniques:

> With a Latin student who was daydreaming, I responded without attempting to punish publicly. As I walked around the room, I opened his book and found the place. Next, I called upon him for answers he knew and praised him.

Dorane Teague, Hoover Middle School, New Mexico, describes how she maintains objectivity:

> When a situation occurs that needs taking care of, I always talk to the student before making any judgments. I listen to his or her side and keep an open mind. I ask "Why?" "How can we change it?" and then work with the student to formulate alternatives.

In summary, effective teachers demonstrate an objective approach, or a nonjudgmental attitude, in the way they maintain discipline and order. Sound classroom management prevents disruption; however, when inappropriate behavior occurs, effective teachers exercise self-control and respond to the total situation rather than reacting to the isolated incident. They act quickly, look for causes rather than blame, gather facts, confer privately and quietly with transgressors, and explore alternatives with students for changing unacceptable behavior. Perhaps most important, effective teachers clearly communicate expected behavior to students at the beginning of the year, inform them of the consequences of disruptive actions, and ensure and demonstrate fair treatment.

Active Listening

A common method for demonstrating concern and attentiveness is a kind of active listening that involves paraphrasing. Aspy (1973) called these paraphrasings "interchangeable responses." Good, Biddle, and Brophy define "interchangeable responses" as

> ...teacher summations of student statements which are interchangeable with what the student has actually said (in other words, teacher responses which show that the teacher has heard and understood the student completely and accurately)(1975, p. 73).

A teacher often begins such a response with a phrase like "What I hear you saying is—," or "Are you saying that—?"

Interchangeable responses provide a kind of mutual feedback on content. The teacher checks the student's comprehension of an idea, and the student checks to see if the response was understood. But interchangeable responses serve an affective function also. The teacher must pay careful attention to catch the nuances and emphases of the student's statement. Such attention implies that the student has something important to say. The teacher is interested in the student and what she or he has to say.

Correlational studies and experimental research data indicate that "improved student gains are a direct result of interchangeable responses by the teachers, rather than some extraneous variable," according to Good et al (1975, pp. 73-74).

A teacher's verbal fluency is obviously an integral part of interchangeable responses. Teachers must be able not only to paraphrase the content, but also to articulate the nuances and implications of the student's statement. And they must be able to do it at a level of language that the student can understand and acknowledge.

Effective teachers demonstrate active "listening" on paper, as well as in classroom interactions (Roueche, 1982). Teacher comments on written work respond to strengths as well as weaknesses, with close attention to nuances and implications. They read "between the lines" and "hear" all the student has said—or tried to say.

Finally, effective teachers sense the mood of the class or individual. As Ornstein and Levine point out, "a shortcoming. . .has been the focus on verbal behavior without considering such nonverbal behaviors as facial expression and gestures" (1981, p. 593). Yet people do sense moods, through verbal interchanges and through nonverbal cues. It's reasonable to assume that teachers and students pay attention to nonverbal behavior. And perhaps effective teachers adjust their plans for the day if they sense that students are depressed or are excited about an upcoming holiday. Many of the effective teachers in a study by Schneider, Klemp, and Kastendiek described interpreting individual nonverbal clues or reading the mood of a group (Schneider et al, 1981). Teachers may even state that they are aware of the feelings, thus providing an "interchangeable response" to emotions.

Excellent teachers are excellent active listeners. They listen to students, both in and out of the classroom, with acceptance before responding. When they do respond, these teachers paraphrase or give other appropriate feedback that reveals understanding of what the student has said. Finally, these teachers encourage students to respect and listen to each other, especially when opinions differ.

Through active listening, our teachers show students that their answers count and are important:

> I invite class participation by the student. All students must treat their classmates with dignity in my classroom— there must be no fear of humiliation by peers (Linda Bergland of Hazen High School, North Dakota).

> When I ask a question, I expect an answer. This often involves waiting, listening, and letting students know their ideas count (Karen Higgins of Oaklea Middle School, Oregon).

> I try to accept any answer to a question as a plausible choice rather than only right or wrong. Any question asked by a student is worth responding to, even if it seems obvious or trivial (Chester Chase of Katahdin High School, Maine).

> Listening involves much more than just hearing what my students say. I begin listening the minute they walk in my classroom door. Their body language tells me when they are having problems. I seem to always know when a student needs some assistance or attention. I try never to be judgmental or overreact, and I use feedback techniques to ensure I have understood (Connie Miller of Spring Valley High School, South Carolina).

> I am a great proponent of "active listening," but in the classroom situation when a student is speaking— either answering or asking a question, I will rephrase his statement, trying to reflect what he has intended. Very often the student has trouble expressing himself. I try to flesh out what he has said. The key to listening

is not to be condescending, but instead to accept each question and each honest attempt to answer as a valid expression of that student's understanding. Very often this feedback has shown me that I was not clear in my directions or statements as I thought I had been. I feel this unthreatening give and take of information—this feedback—is the heart of the art of teaching (Cheryl Otis Nicola of Hazen High School, North Dakota).

Rapport and Empathy

Although rapport, empathy, and active listening are treated in our study as separate entities, all three of these interpersonal skills are closely related and often difficult to distinguish from one another. In fact, rapport and active listening appear to be subsets of the more general term empathy. However, we chose, for the purposes of our study, to define *rapport* as the ability to maintain an approving and mutually favorable relationship with students, and *empathy* as the quality of being aware and accepting of students' thoughts and feelings. Thus, empathy implies a prerequisite awareness and acceptance of students' emotions before a teacher is able to establish rapport with students. Most teachers in our study work to build good rapport with students and are able to empathize with them.

Teachers build rapport by showing respect for students, treating them fairly, and trusting them. Our effective teachers model the behavior that they expect from their students, thus establishing mutual respect between themselves and their students and among the students for each other. Establishing good rapport with students requires that teachers be open and honest with them. Effective teachers care sincerely about their students' interests and share their own personal feelings and experiences. The following excerpts illustrate techniques to establish good rapport:

I think rapport in the classroom is very necessary if there is to be the communication that allows *students to learn and teachers to teach.* There cannot be teaching if there is no learning. Rapport is developed or created, and since this is a relationship between teacher and student, adult and youth, then I, the adult, have the responsibility to try to develop the individual and the classroom rapport that helps to create a healthy learning atmosphere.

To help accomplish this I have one and only one rule that I give my students at the beginning of the school year, and it is as follows: "Every individual in this class is entitled to proper respect from each and every other person in the classroom, including the teacher." To help accomplish this, we must all know that anyone, including this teacher, who shows disrespect to another individual in this classroom will have to apologize to that individual or individuals in front of the group witnessing the disrespectful action.

Sometimes during the first week of school after going over the rule, the students and I discuss it. I let them come up with an interpretation of what it means regarding the teacher's responsibilities and the students' responsibilities. They come up with about every rule that I would ever want, but we do not write them down. We all agree that they are the natural interpretations of the one rule and any high school student could be expected to understand.

The discussion that generally takes about 20 minutes spawns a lot of good comments from students that help me begin to get acquainted with the individuals and lays the foundation for the rapport that I hope develops during the first few weeks of school.

I can remember two occasions when I have had to apologize to the class during the last ten years and two or three times a year I have had to apologize to an individual. There have been two times during the last five years when a student has had to stand before the class and apologize. It was very difficult in both cases; but it was effective in turning around a deteriorating situation and both students were able to successfully complete the year.

This is one of many things I do to develop the rapport that I like to have in my classroom (Harold Piatt, Manzano High School, New Mexico).

Rapport is extremely important. Teachers can make or break the whole school year by how they approach their classes the first week of school. I spend a lot of time the first two days establishing the atmosphere of the class, and it truly pays off. The students must feel that you are on their side both collectively and individually, but they must also have it told to them and then "demonstrated" to them that you will tolerate no funny business in your classroom. The students must know that you are in control of yourself and the classroom, but you are understanding and reasonable. If you can show them this, 95 percent of the students will be with you and the other 5 percent will have no alternative but to conform through sheer peer pressure. This is my secret of discipline and why I can easily control my big 8th graders even through I am only 5'2" and weigh 120 pounds. I never use physical threats and only touch my students to pat them on the back or hug them on the last day of school (Marky Maughan, Soldotna Junior High School, Alaska).

Empathy, as distinguished from rapport, is the ability to put one's self in the place of another in an attempt to understand reality from another's perspective. The teachers in our study adeptly perceive the thoughts and emotions of their young, teenage students who are experiencing many dramatic changes. Warm and caring, they assert high expectations firmly and fairly by laying well-planned paths to success for their students. Some responses from our teachers reveal an empathetic understanding of teenagers' daily problems and dilemmas:

> One student in this teacher's class went totally blank at the start of her AP test and broke into tears. The teacher called her into his office, calmed her down, and had her come back later for the exam. She now has a Ph.D. in chemistry from McGill University (Eldon K. Helm, principal at Cheyenne Mountain High School in Colorado, describing Edward Walford).

> It is often very difficult to suppress my own feelings and reactions to situations and to my students. I have trained myself into their minds and accept their feelings as valid, thereby responding accordingly. This is used most often during an emotional outbreak by a student.
> For example, one of my students protested rather strongly and belligerently about my insisting that he use the computer program on job exploration. (We use a computerized interest survey in which the computer prints out the answers to questions.) I knew this student resisted any talk in class about careers by saying "Who cares? I won't work anyway."
> I had a strong feeling that his vocal resistance was actually a fear that he wouldn't be suited for any job at all; he would then have proof of his feelings of being a failure. I talked to the business teacher who guided the students through the process. He helped this student by suggesting that the student make certain selections which the teacher knew would produce a good list of jobs.
> After his session with the computer, the student strutted back into class boasting a list of 99 jobs for which he was suited! That event was a turning point for him. He seemed not to be as belligerent or as angry at himself or his world. He became a very serious student—intent on graduating, which he did.
> I could very easily have "reacted" to his resistance. But instead I listened "between the words," and that made all the difference (Cheryl Otis Nicola, Hazen High School, North Dakota).

> I feel that anyone who works with people successfully should be able to empathize with others. Perhaps it is even more true for those who work with children or

young people for they are even less able to be always in control of their situation.

For example, they are required by law to be in homes which may be less than desirable and in a classroom situation that may be very frustrating. A student may be struggling with a limited learning ability that he/she does not yet understand. Students need help in understanding these types of problems.

I recall an eighth grade class of about 40 students that I had during my second year as a teacher. I only remember two names from that group, but I shall never forget them. John was an eleven-year-old with an IQ of over 160, and James, age twelve, with an IQ of about 75. John was a brilliant student who was very comfortable with adults but who could not communicate with his peers. James got along with everyone but was aware that he didn't learn as fast as the others. I saw both boys shed tears of frustration as they tried to cope with a situation they did not understand.

John enjoyed being around adults, so I would quite often eat in the cafeteria so that he could eat with me. Generally, another student or two would join us so this seemed to help John get through the day. But in James' situation, the problem of understanding mathematics was not so easily solved or even addressed. Twenty-five years ago special education was not so well defined, and there was no special class for James. I know that I didn't do a very good job of working with James, but I think he appreciated the special attention I gave him after school.

It takes patience to go over and over a particular math concept with a class, and the best source for patience is an empathetic heart. Part of the challenge for me as a teacher is to try to feel what is going on in the student, to anticipate the questions forming in his mind, and try to encourage him or her to verbalize that question. The question needs to be asked so that the answer can be understood.

To me, to be a teacher is to be empathetic. I am excited when a student learns, and I am sad when the learning does not take place. I can hug or give a pat on the back in one situation, and I can wipe a tear out of my eye in another situation. When one of my students fails, then to that degree I have failed.

When I can no longer show empathy with my students, then I will know it is time to retire (Harold Piatt, Manzano High School, New Mexico).

According to Klemp, the interpersonal skills exhibited by these outstanding teachers also characterize people who achieve and succeed in the world of work in general. Effective performers,

Klemp states, demonstrate "accurate empathy," which means they interpret and act on cues that are constantly conveyed by others. The ability to interpret signals accurately from others is particularly useful in a helping profession, such as teaching, because it precipitates experiences that help students.

We refer to our final group of teacher behaviors as cognitive themes—the higher order information-processing skills of understanding, applying, analyzing, and synthesizing. We have identified four general teaching characteristics in the cognitive domain. These characteristics include: individualized perception, teaching strategies, knowledge, and innovation.

Cognitive Skills

We have grouped the four remaining teaching characteristics identified in our study, related to intellectual ability, into the category of cognitive skills. We believe, as Kemp explains, that cognitive skills involve the ability to synthesize information thematically and logically, to understand many sides of a controversial issue, and to learn from experience (Klemp, 1977). Thus, in this section we present four major cognitive teaching themes:

- Individualized perception—response to the individual needs of each student
- Teaching strategies—the techniques used by excellent teachers
- Knowledge
- Innovation.

These cognitive themes describe *what* effective teachers do rather than *how* they perform (as discussed in the section on interpersonal skills).

Individualized Perception

Effective teachers make an effort to find out about their students as individuals, diagnose their needs and learning styles, and then incorporate that knowledge into planned instructional activities.

Sometimes teachers learn about students before the course begins by consulting school records and checking test scores. Once classes begin, these teachers work to learn each student's name quickly. They gather information about each student's needs, abilities, learning styles, interests, and prior learning. They may also use diagnostic tests, questionnaires, observation, or informal conversations. Some effective teachers spend half of the first class day establishing rules, routines, and expectations, and the other half getting to know the students.

Then effective teachers use that information to provide materials and ask questions on an appropriate level. Realizing that a class comprises individuals, these teachers use their knowledge of the students' interests and abilities to draw them into class activities. While the class is indeed a group, many teacher-individual interactions—for example, comments written on individual papers—provide opportunities for individualized feedback, encouragement, and praise.

The teachers in our study offered examples of how they personalize learning programs. Richard Dell'Ergo, John J. Rhodes Junior High School in Arizona, gives one such example:

> I immediately try to assess individual student interests through a written survey that asks students for their favorite pastimes. If a student isn't sparked by the material, I can refer back to these and suggest related activities. For example, a student listed photography as his prime interest. He did an extra-credit assignment by photographing as many examples of government services as he could find on his block. This gave him a successful experience in the class, and his overall work improved sharply.

Effective teachers often provide individualized assignments, especially in long-term projects or homework. These out-of-class assignments can accommodate and provide for a variety of needs, interests, and learning styles. Attention to students as individuals builds rapport because individual worth and importance are affirmed with such attention. These elements of effective teaching are expressed in Principal John Garrison's description of Marilyn Sullivan, Hoover Middle School in New Mexico:

> During the semester the students in the drama classes critique each other's progress; for shy, insecure students she offers physical contact as support (a hug, pat and so on). She also carefully watches that they are not criticized more often than the more popular students. For more secure, advanced students, she encourages more stringent critiques. She uses humor to take the "sting" out of some unpleasant situations.

A problem with individual perceptions lies in the area of expectations. While effective teachers have high expectations for all students, they must recognize differences in prior learning, abilities, needs, and motivations. All teachers have expectations about individuals that are usually accurate. But effective teachers carefully avoid stereotyping students and change their expectations if a student's performance proves differently (Brophy and Good, 1974). They continue to make academic demands and opportunities and don't give up, and they recognize effort and improvement as well as superior performance.

Effective teachers willingly work harder for low-achievers, using more patience, persistence, diagnosis, and remediation. The problem of trying to provide low-achievers with the success they need while trying to provide high-achievers the challenge they need becomes complex and is compounded as students get older, and the gap widens.

Nevertheless, effective teachers facilitate student learning by matching students' entering ability with tasks, and they capitalize on students' personal interests and experiences to capture their attention. Principal George W. Seagraves, Lee County High School in North Carolina, describes how teacher Nancy R. Cope wins students' active participation in learning:

> Students come first! She keeps a small notebook of addresses and phone numbers, calls them at home if something develops that she feels interests a given individual. In return students call her for help, to share, and to get ideas on work. She knows students as individuals and brings special things for each one's interests.

Consequently, effective teachers personalize instructional programs even when meeting with over a hundred students every day. By considering students' values, attitudes, and experiences when making curriculum choices and decisions, effective teachers make learning relevant to the lives of each student.

Teaching Strategies

In our study, we identified six general qualities that characterize the strategies used by effective teachers:

- Skillful and enthusiastic teaching
- Well-organized courses
- Student-centered style
- Careful monitoring and evaluating
- A structured, yet flexible approach
- Active involvement of students.

Because teaching techniques and methods have been the primary foci of much research concerning effective teachers, we have learned a great deal about what works and what does not. Recent studies focus on management of classroom time and establish a high correlation between the time spent on instruction and learning and increased student achievement. The terminology referring to the "time" factor varies, but for now we will use David Berliner's (1979) terms: allocated time, engaged time, and academic learning time.

- *Allocated time* is time planned for the learning task. While allocated time is a necessary pre-condition for learning, it does not guarantee that learning will take place.
- *Engaged time*, sometimes called time-on-task, is the time a student actually spends on the learning task. Engaged time has a positive correlation with achievement, but does not necessarily equate with maximum learning. It merely provides "the opportunity for effective teaching and productive learning" (Rutter et al, 1979).
- *Academic learning time* is the time a student spends on task working at a successful level. Also called ALT, academic learning time is spent in actual learning, not just trying to learn or just re-hashing material previously mastered. Study after study indicates a high correlation between increased ALT and increased achievement.

Although our study focuses only slightly on the time variable, as a discrete learning factor, the facets of our research examining principal characteristics and school climate reveal a major emphasis on learning time in effective schools. In querying principals and teachers about principal behaviors, we discovered considerable effort exerted by everyone in the school and especially by the principal toward careful protection of time spent on learning. Implicit in teachers' descriptions of what they do and how they do it is the assumption that time on task is maximized through sound teaching strategies. We turn now to the six qualities that stand out as recurring characteristics of the teaching techniques demonstrated by excellent teachers:

- Skillful and enthusiastic teaching
- Well-organized classrooms and courses
- Student-centered style
- Monitoring and evaluating
- Structured, yet flexible approach
- Active involvement of students.

**1. Skillful and Enthusiastic Teaching.** Effective teachers are enthusiastic—a characteristic that appears frequently in the literature. Boyer calls for "contagious enthusiasm" (1983, p. 312). Roueche says "it is crucial that the teacher exhibit tremendous excitement" (1982, p. 19). Good, Biddle, and Brophy say effective teachers are enthusiastic and skilled in motivating students and attempt "to generate enthusiasm directly and often" (1975, pp. 59-60). Troisi's summary calls for "enthusiasm," (1979, p. 4) and Morgan describes "a high energy level" (1979, p. 173). According to college students surveyed by Blai, an effective teacher "has an enthusiastic attitude toward the subject" (1982, p. 6). Mosley and Smith's survey of high school students indicates that students like a teacher "who is excited about the subject" (1982, p. 273). Mackenzie says that "any curriculum works better if it is implemented with enthusiasm" (1983, p. 10).

However, we can also imagine the wonderfully enthusiastic teacher who is concerned about individual students but is poorly organized and not quite in control of the classroom. For that teacher, high enthusiasm, as an isolated factor, will be unrelated or negatively correlated to achievement. Like all other factors, enthusiasm interrelates in an appropriate combination with a group of behaviors that characterize effective teachers.

Very little of the teacher literature describes actual "enthusiasm behaviors" that teachers can be trained to exhibit. Troisi mentions an absence of a monotone delivery or deadpan face (1979, p. 4). Roueche mentions modeling, using nonverbal behaviors such as facial expressions and voice quality to convey desired messages (1982, p. 21). And Mackenzie says that rewards for achievement can stimulate interest, and a variety of techniques indicates enthusiasm (1983, p. 10).

Also, an individual teacher may exhibit enthusiasm in a manner unlike anyone else. One may be a formal, dignified teacher of English who quietly exhibits a deep appreciation of literature and draws a similar appreciation from his or her students. Another may be a "fired-up" and often funny math teacher who thinks first-year algebra is the greatest thing that ever happened. Both are enthusiastic about their subjects; and assuming they exhibit other important characteristics, both may be very effective teachers.

Our study supports the conclusion that effective teachers have a high degree of "teacher activism" (Morgan, 1979, p. 163). Jane Stallings points out,

> A teacher can develop concepts with a group and can

> change examples or illustrations to coincide with the
> group's background or experience. If students do not
> understand, the teacher can find yet another example.
> Books or machines do not do that (1981, p. 8)

Effective teachers interact with the class almost constantly. Teacher interaction includes "providing oral instruction for new work, discussing and reviewing students' work, providing drill and practice, asking questions, acknowledging correct responses and supportively correcting wrong responses," according to Stallings. Teachers move around the room during the class, monitoring, helping, explaining, observing. Learning is oriented toward students—their needs, interests, abilities, and their active involvement—but the teacher remains the director of the learning. A high degree of academic teacher-led instruction correlates positively with achievement, many studies show.

2. Well-Organized Classrooms and Courses. The teachers in our study demonstrated effective management of their classrooms and curriculum. They clearly communicate goals and objectives to students, carefully plan learning activities, and maintain an orderly classroom. With these teachers, sound organizational and management skills are so highly interrelated with other behaviors that they are difficult to separate, and they tend to spill over into other areas of our discussion. However, all of the research on effective teaching treats some common behaviors related to classroom and curriculum management—a businesslike attitude, efficient use of time, detailed planning, a variety of activities, high expectations, monitoring and feedback, verbal clarity, and the like. Furthermore, researchers agree that an orderly, safe environment is consistently related to higher student achievement.

There is a dual purpose for strong classroom management: to promote student learning and to prevent student disruption. The theory tends to be cyclical: If students are actively involved in the learning process, they will not be disruptive; they will remain on task. If they become bored, restless, frustrated, or confused, they get off-task and often disrupt others. Effective classrooms, according to Ronald Edmonds, are "orderly without being rigid, quiet without being disruptive, and generally conducive to the instructional business at hand" (1979, p. 22). Gail Oliver, Taft Middle School in New Mexico, illustrates efficient classroom management skills:

> The student is first. I feel confident in stressing this.
> Learning styles are varied, but a teacher can have a
> management system that allows children to learn in a

way that's best suited to them. I am a task-oriented person; my classroom represents this.

Effective teachers plan in detail. They plan a variety of activities at differing levels so that students don't become bored, restless or frustrated.

They plan routine procedures—how and when to turn in homework; how to get permission to leave the room; how to get students quiet; how to deal with tardies, chewing gum, lost pencils; and so on.

They plan the physical arrangement of the room with students in mind. Are materials easily accessible? Can the teacher get close enough to students to monitor and help them individually? Can all students see the chalkboard, lectern, or screen?

They plan and organize materials—handouts, questions for a teacher-led discussion, topics for a composition assignment, the numbers of the questions to be assigned.

They plan for interactions. Will this be noisy activity? How will students form groups? Will we need to move some of the furniture?

They frequently plan oral instructions and explanations *in advance*, especially if the situation is new and/or complex. Many teachers have a "Just-in-Case" plan in mind, or even tucked into a drawer or closet—just in case they need more practice, just in case they finish early, just in case the teacher gets sick, just in case the unexpected occurs. In other words, they think *all the way through* a lesson and plan for the expected and the unexpected.

Linda Rottman, John J. Rhodes Junior High School in Arizona, conveys awareness and understanding of the critical impact thorough planning has on effective teaching:

> "Paying attention to detail" is the key to introducing ideas, programs, or techniques to the students. Being well prepared with goals and the steps necessary to accomplish those goals will ensure success, provided the idea has merit. Students need to see the value of a new program before they will buy ownership into it.

Even with a plan, effective teachers remain flexible. Plans are not written in stone; and if the unexpected occurs—a spontaneous discussion, an unannounced fire drill, a triumph or tragedy in the class—the teacher incorporates that occurrence into the plan and adjusts.

Effective teachers start off with a carefully planned bang. On the first day, they make expectations clear with explicit oral instructions, establish rules and routines and explain the course objectives, grading criteria, and expectations for learning tasks and behavior. At the college level and often on the secondary, expectations and objectives may be written. They quite often hand out a syllabus that includes objectives, a list of assignments and deadlines, and perhaps examples of acceptable formats for assignments and activities. They are businesslike, efficient, clearly task-oriented.

Then effective teachers follow up. In the first few weeks, they may actively teach routines by demonstrating, modeling, providing practice, monitoring, and providing corrective feedback. They enforce rules, routines and deadlines, usually working with the class as a whole until routines are established, even if small-group or individualized work is going to be part of later activities. Because rules and routines are established early, effective teachers maintain an orderly, task-oriented environment with little apparent effort.

We also noted some behaviors that are constant throughout the course. While people can be trained to perform these activities, many of them occur simultaneously and, for the effective teacher, almost automatically. Most of these behaviors fit both sides of the dual academic/behavioral goal of classroom management.

• They provide for *continuity of the lesson.* Transitions from one activity to the next are smooth and waste little time. Instructions are clear. Materials are available and quickly distributed. Organizational tasks are usually handled as part of established routines. Billups and Rauth indicate that effective teachers have only three to six formal rules, but 30 to 50 routine procedures (1984, p. 37). They avoid interrupting the instructional flow—for example, suddenly remembering and calling for the homework assignment when students have just begun a new activity.

• They set a brisk pace and keep the momentum going. If students spend too much time on a long or repetitive task, they become bored and often disruptive. A planned variety of activities maintain active student involvement and learning.

• They remain in control of the class, even when activities are student-centered through moving around the room frequently, monitoring student performances, and providing specific feedback and teacher interaction. These teachers demand the students' attention. They follow through on assignments and procedures and provide materials for early finishers. Students are expected and helped to complete their work successfully and to use time constructively.

• They also provide for some quiet time. Rutter et al noted that the more successful schools in their study "had periods of quiet work when teachers expected students to work in silence" (1979, p. 17).

• Finally, effective teachers model the behaviors they expect. They are punctual, well-organized, and do not waste time. They stay on task, are businesslike and do not interrupt the learning task. Attentive to the room's appearance, they model care for materials, displays, orderly shelves, and cleanliness. They are friendly and attentive to individual needs, and make it clear that they expect a like behavior from the students.

3. Student-Centered Style. While excellent teachers do structure and guide the learning process, emerging evidence supports the notion that teaching is more effective when it is student-centered, rather than teacher- or subject-centered (Knowles, 1975). That is, curriculum is developed to meet the needs of the students rather than to reflect the teacher's preference or pet interests.

The teachers in our study demonstrate a student-centered approach. They are concerned about maintaining a high student success rate, especially when introducing new material or assigning new, unfamiliar tasks. Their supportive classroom atmosphere indicates that, to them, students count and are, indeed, important. They work to ensure that course content and assignments are relevant and useful to students' lives and futures, and encourage independent thinking and the expression of alternative viewpoints in open dialogue on controversial or multifaceted issues. And of course, they reinforce students and support them in their efforts.

Principal Richard F. Lindgren, Illing Junior High School in Connecticut, depicts a sense of student-centeredness in art teacher, Donna Fitzgerald:

> She provides positive encouragement and stresses the importance of the learning process rather than the visual product. She is constantly displaying the student's work in the school and in the community to further encourage her students to learn and experiment. Success breeds success. She is quick to praise an accomplishment no matter how small it is.

Although this quality of student-centered learning is not a subject of explicit discussion in the research studies we have mentioned it is an implied concept in most. Pat Cross suggests that student-centered learning will be a trend of the 1980s in higher education (1977); our excellent secondary teachers reflect this theme in their teaching strategies.

4. Monitoring and Evaluating. Effective teachers provide frequent, specific feedback, mixed with praise, little criticism, and much neutral acknowledgement. Nearly every study of effective teaching speaks to the importance of monitoring and feedback.

Teachers must monitor student's performances to know if they are learning successfully. They may do so using verbal interaction, nonverbal clues, quizzes, and homework checks—to mention a few. They may call on students or scan the room, checking for appropriate materials and behavior. They may ask questions, paraphrasing student responses to check comprehension.

Through monitoring, teachers receive feedback on the success of their lesson. With older or high-achieving students in a supportive environment, the teachers may even ask directly "Is that point clear?" or "Do you understand how this works?" and trust the answers. But teacher-led discussion or supervised practice, either written or oral, is more reliable, and effective teachers check frequently to see that students understand.

Monitoring is especially important for low-achievers, for they often do not ask for feedback or clarification. They do not want to look "dumb" and lose their self-respect or the respect of their peers. At the same time, however, they cannot tell how they are doing unless the teacher monitors and provides feedback (Good, 1982).

Feedback is an obvious corollary of monitoring. Students need to know about their progress, and to be constructive, feedback should be specific, frequent, and congruent, attending to both the strengths and weaknesses of the student's work. Teachers may use "structuring" comments, such as hints or reminders, to help the students achieve the objectives. Some feedback takes the form of simple acknowledgements or encouragement that a student is doing okay or is on the right track. Corrective feedback, when a student is not doing well, must be specific, frequent, and positive to be helpful (Stallings, 1980, 1981). Again, structuring comments often helps students see the way to success. Simple negative feedback may be helpful, but its effect is dramatically improved when corrective information is also provided (Easton, 1983-84; Schneider et al, 1981). However, Brophy says:

> . . . it should be noted that overt feedback from the teacher is not always necessary. In social learning situations, learners tend to assume they are correct unless explicitly informed otherwise. This tendency probably is reinforced in most classrooms by corresponding teacher behaviors during recitations (1981, p. 6).

Feedback, like monitoring, may take many forms. One is obviously oral interaction between the teachers and students. Another is in the form of grading. Frequent quizzes, graded by the teacher, provide both monitoring for the teacher and feedback for the students. Of course, to be helpful, papers must be graded and returned quickly, so that the feedback can be used by the student to further the learning process. For both monitoring and feedback, researchers recommend that some homework be graded. Written comments on papers, if specific and congruent, can also be helpful. Obviously teachers need to keep accurate records of grades, and some studies show that specific feedback to parents is also helpful.

Teachers also monitor and provide feedback by asking questions that are at an appropriate level of difficulty. Students should find that learning is possible and relatively painless, that they can understand and respond to most questions successfully, and that they can complete independent assignments correctly (Brophy, 1979). However, 100 percent success is not advisable. If all students maintain a 100 percent success rate, they are "overlearning" and wasting time on material they have already mastered (Good et al, 1975, p. 77). In fact, a too high success rate may lead to poor performance; students get careless or bored (Squires et al, 1979).

Maxine Moore, Spartanburg High School in South Carolina, demonstrates understanding of appropriate questioning and feedback techniques in the following excerpt:

> When a student answers a question incorrectly, instead of saying "No," I help him to find an acceptable answer, give him clues, probe his mind, and allow him to feel he has contributed to the class.

PRAISE AND CRITICISM IN THE CLASSROOM. Praise and criticism cannot be classified as feedback. Brophy defines "praise" in its usual sense: "to commend the work of or to express approval or admiration" (1981, p. 5). He clarifies this definition:

> [Praise] connotes a more intense or detailed teacher response to student behavior than terms such as "feedback" or "affirmation of correct response" do. When teachers praise students, they do not merely tell them the degree of success they achieved (by nodding or repeating answers, by saying "okay," "right," or "correct," or by giving a letter grade or percentage score). In addition to such feedback, praise statements express positive teacher affect (surprise, delight, excitement) and/or place the student's behavior in context by giving information about its value or its implications about the student's status (pp. 5-6).

He goes on to say that

> . . . praise and criticism must be distinguished from simple (affectively neutral) feedback, and also from more global attributes such as "warmth" or "hostility." The latter terms describe generalized attitudes or emotional states, although they may include praise and criticism as partial manifestations (p. 6).

The *frequency* of praise is not as strong a correlate with high achievement as is *appropriate use* of praise and the absence of excessive or abusive criticism (Good et al, 1975). Brophy (1981) explains that praise, in order to be appropriate, must be specific, contingent, and credible. While general praise contributes to the environment and may be a motivator, praise—like feedback—must be specific to be effective and close to the event—praise for a paper written three weeks ago occurs too late. According to Rutter and colleagues, formal prizes, such as once-a-year pins or certificates, do not serve as valuable reinforcers because they are not contingent on the event, there are too few of them, and they are given too infrequently (1979).

Praise must also be credible. If teachers praise many students frequently, the praise loses its value and no longer sounds sincere. It should be varied and spontaneous.

Low-ability students, with their backgrounds of frequent failure, respond more favorably to praise than high ability students, according to many studies. Good's studies about teacher expectations indicate that some teachers are excessively protective and sympathetic to low-achievers; therefore, they praise marginal answers and make few demands (1982). Other teachers seem intolerant: they criticize low-achievers more frequently, offer fewer opportunities for response, and provide feedback that is less specific and less frequent (Good, 1981). Low-achievers need praise for their successes; but the praise should be specific, contingent on the behavior, sincere, and tempered by the relative infrequency and simple feedback that high-achievers receive.

CRITICISM. Although rarely helpful, criticism can be interpreted as a demand for excellence and a signal of high expectations. Gage cites a study in which the "most effective teachers gave criticism only a small percentage of the time (about 2 percent), and only with pupils of higher socioeconomic status, while the less effective teachers *never* gave such criticism" (1978, p. 234). Corrective, but affectively neutral, feedback and structuring comments relate directly to achievement, but criticism that goes beyond simple feedback to express disapproval or rejection most likely results in both lower self-concept and achievement. Criticism may also result in student withdrawal from learning activities; the student doesn't want to risk failure and criticism, so he or she becomes a "passive" learner (Good, 1982).

Two principals from our study offer representative descriptions of teachers who demonstrate ease and facility in using appropriate corrective feedback:

> Young people are often fragile and tentative, especially responding in class. She always tries to encourage participation in class and values the students' answers, never ridicules a student for an incorrect response, but tries to teach from that error and turn it into a positive experience for the students (Nancy Brazier Green's methods described by Loretta Collier, principal of Booker T. Washington High School, Oklahoma).

> Marilyn Sullivan often takes a student's idea, expands on it, sets the idea in motion, and gives the student full credit for what happened with his or her idea (Sullivan, a teacher at Hoover Middle School, described by John Garrison, principal).

5. Structured, Yet Flexible Approach. Effective teachers plan a variety of activities including lecture, discussion, written or oral drill, group work, student recitation, various electronic media, and others. No one of these methods is inherently better than the others; all can be effective. Variety is the important consideration.

Effective teachers match the techniques to the situation: younger students or older ones, a large class or a small one, a heterogeneous group or a homogeneous one, basic skills or complex problemsolving, and so on. They recognize that the same techniques do not work with everyone all the time and look at the lesson objectives, selecting appropriate techniques.

For example, studies show that "direct instruction" techniques are successful in teaching basic skills. Direct instruction includes a strong academic focus, a teacher-centered focus, limited student choice of activity, use of large groups (the class as a whole) rather than small ones, and use of factual questions and controlled practice (Rosenshine, 1979). Most students learn basic skills and study habits in the elementary grades, where direct instruction techniques have been most effective (Good et al, 1975).

However, as students master basic skills, more "indirectness" becomes appropriate. Goals become more complex and numerous; teachers ask more open questions, aiming to foster higher-level thinking skills such as application or analysis. Students have more choices and may, with teacher guidance, modify their assignments to match their own needs and interests better. Ruth Nicholson, Irmo High School in South Carolina, reveals a sense of "indirectness" by sequencing progressively more complex tasks in order to develop higher level skills:

> Activities that are challenging, but not impossible, help students to learn. By sequencing these activities from the simple to the more complex, I can guide students to comprehend the information and assimilate it. By developing tasks at various levels of thinking and in all types of learning modes, I make certain that there is something to spark each type of student.

Variety stimulates student interest and prevents boredom. Students remain actively involved in learning, which is important for both achievement and classroom management. Variety allows for students' different learning styles.

The following selections represent the variety of methods we find among our teacher participants in their approach to teaching:

> A variety of styles and methods must be used, since students learn in different ways. Question and answer sequences are built into lectures to maintain student interest. The Socratic method is constantly used. Challenging readings, thought-provoking movies, small group problem-solving activities, and lifelike debates and simulations stimulate students to learn (David Arnold, Clay Junior High School, Indiana).

> After a trip with Mrs. Deal to a local wilderness area, students were asked to describe their feelings about the trip. One student confessed she had never seen anything quite so beautiful as the 200-year-old trees and hoped no one would ever cut those trees. All the reading in a textbook about saving natural resources would not have made such an impression. She had actually "seen" what she had been reading about and the impression would last forever (Sharon Deal, described by W. Ben Nesbit, principal of Spring Valley High School, South Carolina).

> Judy has always been ready to try new ideas in her classroom, whether the ideas involve the students doing research for debate on the causes of World War I or writing concrete poetry to describe the United States at a certain period of time in history.
> Her bulletin boards reflect student ideas, which are frequently discussed in the classroom. Students' suggestions for activities are well received. She takes her students to the legislature and to museums on field trips. Her classes are involved in roleplaying and heated,

though intelligent and sound, logically-backed discussions. Her students have participated at St. John's College in seminars on The Declaration of Independence.

To "turn-on" students, she uses records and sheet music to have class sing-alongs, which the students have thoroughly enjoyed. She has written puppet shows that her students have performed for community groups. Her students have become involved enough to investigate issues and write letters and make telephone calls to state legislators. Her classes are enlivened by cultural days, full of music, food, and fun, as well as relevant history (Judith Cole's teaching methods, as described by J.A. Krueger, principal, Manzano High School, New Mexico).

As we pointed out earlier, flexibility is also an important aspect of teacher effectiveness. The following responses illustrate the kind of flexibility and spontaneity in teaching we find in our sample:

> Each day is a new chance to work with students. When they arrive in class, their attitudes differ from day to day. It is important to get a "feel for the weather" before I start teaching each class. I have specific plans, but I have to adjust them to fit the situations that exist. Experience and a love for young people are the best guides (L.D. Naegelin of Winston Churchill High School, Texas).

> Monitoring and adjusting is a vital part of my total teaching act. Through total group response and individual sampling I can get the picture of where the class is and what they need and adjust accordingly (Ruth Ann Nicholson of Irmo High School, South Carolina).

> In addition to incorporating new ideas I have garnered from study or conversing with others, I also capitalize on what happens spontaneously in a given class. Sometimes a student's comment or my own reaction to comments during discussions will prompt me to incorporate the idea into the next class presentation. Thereby, what was spontaneous in one situation becomes planned into the next situation (Sandra Key of Jonesboro High School, Arkansas).

6. Active Involvement of Students. Many researchers consider "student involvement" a critical variable of effective teaching. And teachers should be involved with the students—leading the discussion, monitoring seatwork, demonstrating how to work a problem, sitting in on small groups, and the like.

Teachers promote active student involvement. They ask a lot of questions. Students who expect to be called on remain alert and attentive. If students do not participate, the teacher rephrases the questions, changes the topic, or tries another technique. By asking questions, teachers monitor student learning and clarify or reteach unclear points. Skilled questioners *probe* for answers, *rephrase questions, ask questions at different levels* of thinking, and *wait* long enough for students to think before answering.

In a discussion, the teachers elicit comments and questions from students, follow up on them, often praise them, and use them to elicit still more responses. However, "eliciting them in the first place seems to be the crucial variable here, not praising them or integrating them into the discussion" (Brophy, 1979, p. 36). Students who actively discuss and review material have higher achievement than those who do not (Stallings, 1981).

Marilyn Sullivan, Hoover Middle School in Albuquerque, New Mexico, illustrates one of the questioning techniques offered by teachers in our study:

> In class situations, I begin by asking easy questions first, those that require answers on the level of concrete knowledge; and I try to let shy or the less-bright students get in on answering these. Then as I progress to asking more difficult questions, I try to pin the brighter students into answering them. I also have lots of questions that have no "right" or "wrong" answers, and these can lead the class into wonderful discussions. Sometimes I argue for one side; then I switch and go to the other side of the questions just to get them thinking.

Effective teachers also foster student involvement by helping students understand the objectives of an activity or the course in general. Students who understand the importance of a task are more likely to get involved, even more so if they see the relevance to their individual goals. Effective teachers make sure that students understand the importance and relevance of an assignment, so that it is not seen as "busywork" (Strother, 1984, p. 425).

Sandra Key, Jonesboro High School in Arkansas, shares her example of these practices:

> I provide my students with written goals at the beginning of the year; they are placed in each student's notebook. Furthermore, at the beginning of each unit students are given concrete objectives; and before each examination the objectives are reviewed. I also place daily objectives on the chalkboard.

A variety of stimulating, lively activities also increases interest, and effective teachers may use suspense, novelty, and often humor to that end. Even simple lectures can stimulate interest, and lively discussions with high participation interest those involved and may intrigue those who listen. Teachers who present material in stimulating ways interest high school and college students.

Harold Piatt's response summarizes well how an effective teacher involves students in learning:

> The first step in stimulating students to learn is to get the students involved in teaching-learning *performance*. With 30 tenth-graders in a geometry class, it takes all the training, talent, energy, and creativity that I have and then some to get every student involved; but I feel that the student's involvement must take place if he or she is going to respond, to feel, to learn.
>
> The lecture becomes a discussion and demonstration. The demonstration involves students whenever possible, and the teacher leads and directs it from all over the classroom and not from behind the desk or podium.
>
> I prefer not to let my students predict what I am going to do or how I am going to present the topics. I do not want myself or the students to get in a rut. How a teacher schedules tests, minitests, quizzes, or daily assignments can be effective in stimulating students to learn.
>
> It helps me to keep the proper perspective if I remember that I have taught only if a student has learned, and I have been successful if every student in my class has responded and has learned (Piatt, teacher in Manzano High School, New Mexico).

Students learn by doing; they use and interact with materials, such as texts, notes, TV, or computers. Teachers serve as facilitators so that students use the materials effectively. "Doing" may involve interacting with other people as well and often involves practice. Effective teachers provide ample opportunities for practice, first with direct teacher supervision and then independently (Gage, 1978).

In conclusion, effective teachers win over students by using a combination of techniques. They are themselves deeply involved in what they do daily in the classroom. For the best, no two days are alike; they:

—Approach each day with enthusiasm
—Run well-organized classes
—Show sincere concern for students
—Monitor and evaluate them accurately and honestly
—Are structured, yet flexible in their approach

—Use a variety of methods that involve students actively in the learning process.

Knowledge

We find only rare mention of this teaching theme in the research on effective teaching (for example, Schneider et al, 1981; Good et al, 1975; Baker et al, 1983). Perhaps, one can speculate, having knowledge of the subject matter and of educational techniques are considered basic to teaching and, therefore, not necessarily distinguishing characteristics of excellent teachers.

Nevertheless, all the teachers in our study continually engage in professional development, thus presenting and considering themselves as a lifelong learners who value the learning process itself. Furthermore, they talk about their own learning and perpetual renewal of knowledge with zest and enthusiasm. For them, as for every professional, seeking new knowledge and refreshing what has already been acquired remains integral to their teaching commitment. The following statement from Stacey Savage-Brooks, Louis Armstrong Middle School in New York, illustrates the high regard our excellent teachers express for learning itself:

> Seneca taught that for as long as we live we must go on learning how to live. DaVinci said that the proper activity for all good men is the pursuit of knowledge, for without knowledge nothing can be loved. Living, learning, and loving are therefore a unity, and teaching is merely modeling that unity for children to emulate. I share my experiences with my students to point out that I, too, am an unfinished product that undergoes constant change, failure, and refinement.

This zeal for learning distinguishes outstanding teachers in a study conducted by Schneider, Klemp, and Kastendiek; they found that effective teachers of adult students differed in their outlook toward learning from average teachers: "while the average faculty members espoused an appreciation for humanistic education, virtually none described themselves as directly engaged in developmental learning," as did the effective teachers (1981, p. 22).

In addition to the usual resources—conferences, workshops, colleagues, and professional literature—the teachers in our study seek knowledge from people in the community who are involved in careers related to their subject matter and from other external sources. That is, art teachers invite other artists into their classes; business teachers take their classes to local personnel offices; language teachers travel, bringing back slides and artifacts;

English teachers schedule poetry readings; and social studies teachers sponsor visits to city and state offices.

This attitude toward lifelong learning is clearly evident in these excerpts:

> Science is an area where keeping up-to-date is a constant struggle. New ideas, methods, and materials are found in periodicals for the most part. I subscribe to ten popular and professional publications and read them thoroughly. Workshops and inservice meetings are also a good source of new ideas. An interchange of ideas with other teachers is particularly useful, but not always possible (Charles Fitzsimmons of Simon Perkins Middle School, Ohio).

> As I attend rehearsals of two professional orchestras three evenings each week, the opportunity to "brainstorm" new ideas, share problems and seek solutions with many excellent public school and individual private music teachers is enriching. It is essential that I continue to grow as a musician and human being (Jean Stevens of Davidson Middle School, California).

> I have remained open to change, to new ideas, and to new approaches to learning. On a sabbatical leave, I lived in Spain, attended a Spanish language school, lived with a non-English speaking family. I became aware of common learning problems faced by students. I have earned well over 100 units of credit in subject areas that have taught me new techniques, methods, and communication tools necessary for continued teaching (Barbara Belluomini of Davidson Middle School, California).

Innovation

Although the quality of searching for new concepts and techniques is infrequently mentioned in literature regarding effective teaching, we noted that it was an identifiable element to effective teaching in our study. Our teachers talk animatedly about change to improve student learning and about taking risks in an attempt to find and adopt new approaches to enhance teaching effectiveness. They search diligently for new and current information and then work systematically to incorporate worthwhile innovations into their classrooms. These teachers demonstrate a commitment to change anything that doesn't work or to improve existing good programs to make them better.

Victoria Brock, Westchester Middle School in Indiana, offers an example:

> As a risk taker, I tend to try new ideas and tech-
> niques regularly. I do not have an easily bruised ego with
> students. If an idea doesn't work, I do not feel threatened;
> I just don't try that one again with that student or group.
> I move on to something else that may work. I keep trying
> different approaches to learning until I hit on a method
> that works with the individuals I am dealing with. Kids
> will tell you if you are off base or if something is
> "boring." Boring is the dreaded word. Upon hearing
> that, I immediately change methods, no matter where I
> am. I cannot accept the idea that learning can be
> "boring."

A commitment to personal growth is evident among the teachers we queried. They work to integrate new and relevant knowledge into their daily teaching. For instance, Vickie Todd, Wasatch
Middle School in Utah, illustrates the ability to put information
and experience into new configurations:

> Gaining knowledge is not as important as using it.
> For every class or program I participate in, I set a goal
> to find at least one idea that can be adapted for my
> classroom....Sometimes good education is trial-and-error.
> error.

In addition, excellent teachers take time to reflect on the
changes they propose and avoid change for the sake of change. Don
Ribbing, Parkway West High School in Missouri, demonstrates
the kind of meticulous and thoughtful approach to innovation
many exhibit:

> I try to avoid radical changes. Refinement of tech-
> niques over time allows for greater control. For example,
> a new writing program is in its second year for one class.
> I see it as a process which will be ongoing as it is adjusted
> to meet the needs of each class and as I search for ways
> to make it more productive.

Finally, principal John Fink, Wyoming High School in Ohio,
describes in Tom Kessinger the types of innovations we have discovered among superior teachers. The following excerpt reveals an
awareness of the critical need for teachers to stay abreast of new
developments in technology and to approach controversial, yet
topical, subjects with an open mind:

> Tom frequently tries new ideas and techniques. He
> helped design and implement a new non-Western
> cultures course for ninth grade students. He's adopted the
> microcomputer for use in several classrooms involving

the teaching of cultures and American government. He's also taken new materials on controversial issues/topics and has woven them into all courses taught within the social studies department. (Within the last five years, he has won an award for showing how economics can be taught to students innovatively.)

Conclusion

We have attempted in our study to identify what motivates good teaching, to discover the interpersonal traits that work for them in building meaningful relationships with individuals and groups of students, and, finally, to describe the intellectual skills that result in sound teaching. In effect, we have presented a composite profile of the characteristics we find among outstanding teachers. It is not a recipe, nor will every person express the qualities we have described in the same manner. But by illustrating the many varieties of teachers—using quotations and highlighting recurring themes and similarities—we propose to share with all individuals involved in teaching now and in the future descriptions of outstanding performers who are presently accomplishing great teaching both in and out of their classrooms. We contend that anyone with reasonable intelligence who wants to become a good or better teacher can cultivate the attributes that characterize excellent teaching.

From our study we conclude, overwhelmingly, that people make a difference. Teachers and principals who excel at what they do and act with strong conviction and deep commitment make a difference in the lives of students. Dedicated to the task of educating, they place high value on learning—and learning how to learn—as a means of developing students to their greatest potential.

Excellent teaching thrives best in an atmosphere that supports and nurtures shared values focused on the central purpose of learning. Leadership is a key ingredient in fostering a school climate conducive to the development of human potential. Hence, our study examined three components: school climate, school leadership attributes, and teacher behaviors found in schools selected for success indicated in concrete outcomes.

With this study we hope to improve the selection and development of people in education. We believe that better selection and development will help bring about the realization of many of the recommendations made by the numerous commissions on the state of affairs in our educational system. We believe that our study has helped identify the goals and outcomes that should result from a process aimed at developing effective, dedicated educators.

School Climate

In our study, we learned that examining an individual school in terms of its overall environment, its shared values, its shared beliefs, and its personality provides accurate insight into how the school affects the students, teachers, and administrators who give it life as an organization. The individual climate of a school becomes the end-product of countless decisions made daily by those—teachers, administrators, and support staff—in charge. More important, this climate makes the difference between the success or failure of the school and its students.

Unfortunately, effective school climate cannot develop from a single formula. No single factors predict high levels of student success or high scores on national tests. Schools represent incredibly complex environments in which forces pull and push, act and react. It is unlikely that any single formula for success will ever be applicable to all schools. In fact, some researchers in the past have argued that the variables of socioeconomic status, family background, personal motivation really account for student success and are uniformly beyond the control of the school in the first place. But this attitude of personal and organizational helplessness is being refuted by a new group of researchers who argue, as do we, that schools can be a place where teachers, administrators, and parents individually and collectively make a difference in the lives of their students. Our study and others indicate that the success of a school in achieving student academic and personal development is not a product of external variables, like race or income level, but of in-school decisions consciously made by those responsible for its academic program.

The literature generated by other researchers and the data produced in our study indicate that specific attitudes, approaches, policies, and decisions can lead to a climate of success within an individual school. Taken together, these actions and decisions constitute a hospitable, inviting climate in which students grow and achieve. That is, outstanding student performance results from a composite, interwoven pattern of attitudes, policies, and behaviors, all consciously designed to shape the entire learning environment of a school or school district. These patterns of policies and behaviors usually interact within the individual school building to create an ever-present learning climate. Indeed, they point to specific climate variables that appear to affect both student and school success. The characteristics we have found common to successful schools are: order, purpose, and coherence; student centeredness; efficiency and objectivity; an atmosphere of optimism and high expectations; and organizational health.

Administrative Leadership

As have other researchers, we discovered that effective schools have effective leaders. As well, we found that the Peters and Waterman attributes, which characterize the best companies, also define qualities of excellence in effective schools. The leadership assessment instrument was designed to determine the extent to which the same leader attributes were common among the principals participating in our study.

In studying the principals of the 33 secondary schools identified by the Department of Education, we noted seven qualities that parallel the Peters and Waterman properties.

1. Flexibility in autonomy and innovation
2. Cohesiveness within the organization
3. Commitment to school mission
4. Recognition of staff
5. Problem solving through collaboration
6. Effective delegation
7. Focus on teaching and learning.

Neither we nor Peters and Waterman have found anything startling or new in the seven attributes we identified. Yet we find that while leaders of corporations and schools quickly state that "people" are their most important asset, we as a society have done little to recognize or reward excellent individuals or to identify and study the behavior of exceptional performers.

Teaching Excellence

In our review of the research literature on teaching effectiveness, we found overwhelming evidence to suggest that, just as a principal makes a difference in affecting school climate and teacher expectations, teachers make the difference in establishing classroom climate. Research soundly documents that one set of specific teacher behaviors does not apply to all teaching situations. Teaching and learning are both interactive and complex. Further, a wide variety of forces at work in a given classroom ultimately determine the type of teacher behavior that is best.

We began our study with the premise that teachers are the key variables in the teaching and learning process. Although earlier studies, such as the Coleman Report, analyzed schoolwide data that neutralized the effect of any one teacher's performance, subsequent research has determined that teachers do make a dramatic difference in student achievement. This finding led us to study exactly *how* exceptional teachers teach and if their teaching is different from that of typical faculty. We have discovered that exceptional teachers manage classrooms and create learning climates in which there is minimal student disruption and smooth transition from one activity to the next. These teachers differ greatly from average faculty in their strong emphasis on "time on task." They are academically focused and absolutely in charge of their classrooms. They select goals, clearly communicate them to students, intervene to keep students moving toward the goal, and carefully monitor programs that are appropriately sequenced. They promote extensive interaction within the classroom and provide immediate feedback and reinforcement to students. Finally, excellent teachers are task-oriented and focus on student achievement.

A Portrait of Excellence

As we completed our research, we began to see an emerging portrait that is quite different from the more traditional picture of teaching. While researchers have tended to focus on a particular aspect or a quality of teaching, such as time on task, activity in any classroom is extraordinarily complex. Interactions occur between teachers and students and among students. Teachers act both ways—formally and informally, through interactions focused on the personal concerns of learners. A wide variety of teaching materials, teaching styles, and learning activities affect what happens in the classroom. Finally, the teacher plays a dual role of teacher and manager.

Researchers have found the classroom to be a rich environment for investigation. In classroom settings, teachers plan what is to occur from an instructional perspective. Some of what is planned is visible in the classroom; some is not. Primarily because values, beliefs, and attitudes are antecedents, rather than visible attributes, much that is critical to the understanding of teaching as an influence process is invisible. George O. Klemp believes that the competence of a person is judged by his or her overall performance. He defines competency as a generic knowledge, skill, trait, self-schema, or motive of a person that is *causally* related to effective behavior. And, further, he proposes that this effective behavior can be measured by referencing it to some external performance criteria (1979).

For our purposes, Klemp draws a useful analogy. He compares a competency to a tool. Both may be used to operate on different situations with different results. Just as the nature of the tool is not overtly evident in the finished product, but only implied, so too is the nature of a competency seldom evident in observed behavior. Hence the Behavioral Event Interview Technique (BEIT), employed in our study, is designed to elicit from subjects underlying attitudes, values, and beliefs that foster competencies leading to effective performance. Having settled on the 12 SRI teaching themes, we sought to provide the exceptional teachers we identified with definitions of the themes and ask them to relate examples or scenarios of their behavior in critical teaching situations. From teachers' self analyses and principals' descriptions of teachers, we formulated the effective teaching model. With some modification our data support the original 12 teaching themes or competencies characterizing excellent teachers with which we began.

The Excellence Axis

We assume that excellent schools seek to produce learners who achieve at their maximum potential. Our research documents strong relationships between organizational climate, administrative leadership, and teaching excellence. These three institutional attributes become synergistic when everyone in the institution contributes to a climate of excellence. We are convinced that excellence in schools occurs in a climate where there is:

- Orderliness
- A sense of purpose
- Efficiency
- Concern for students
- Optimism
- An emphasis on quality.

Second, it is obvious that administration exists to establish and manage a climate that is satisfying and rewarding. We are pleased to find that the effective principals we identified exhibit behavior similar to the innovative leaders in the Peters and Waterman study. Excellent leadership is relatively the same whether it occurs in McDonald's or in America's public schools. Although there are distinct differences in the expectations and environments between schools and profit-making organizations, basic human behavior interactions among individuals remain quite similar.

Third, we feel that our study has been able to discover a rich set of teacher behaviors that describe well the essence of teaching. Although we have expanded the SRI descriptions, our findings regarding exceptional teachers are supported by thousands of research projects conducted in teaching and learning environments across the teaching spectrum, from elementary to graduate schools.

Finally, our emphasis has been on the climate characteristics, administrative principles, and teaching behaviors that produce student achievement in schools. Our developmental model seeks to link climate, administrative leadership, and teacher excellence to measurable growth and development in the learner. Thus, the excellence axis seeks to increase effort and motivation in the learner and further conveys the message that effort leads to performance and that performance leads to the attainment of important goals. The essence of excellent teaching is to provide strong leadership along the axis to excellence in the life of the learner.

SCHOOLS SELECTED BY USDE SECONDARY SCHOOL RECOGNITION PROGRAM, 1982-83

AGUA FRIA UNION HIGH SCHOOL
530 East Riley Dr.
Avondale, AZ 85323

ALBUQUERQUE HIGH SCHOOL*
800 Odelia Road, NE
Albuquerque, NM 87102

AMES SENIOR HIGH SCHOOL
20th and Ridgewood
Ames, IA 50010

AMITY REGIONAL JUNIOR HIGH SCHOOL
Ohman Ave.
Orange, CT 06477

AMITY REGIONAL SENIOR HIGH SCHOOL*
25 Newton Road
Woodbridge, CT 06525

ANNIE CAMP MIDDLE SCHOOL*
1307 Flint St.
Jonesboro, AR 72401

ARDMORE HIGH SCHOOL
PO Box 1709
Ardmore, OK 73402

BATON ROUGE HIGH SCHOOL
2825 Government St.
Baton Rouge, LA 70806

BEATRICE SENIOR HIGH SCHOOL
215 North 5th St.
Beatrice, NE 68310

BENJAMIN FRANKLIN JUNIOR HIGH SCHOOL
1420 North 8th St.
Fargo, ND 58102

BLOOMFIELD HILLS LASHER HIGH SCHOOL
3456 Lasher Road
Bloomfield Hills, MI 48013

BLUE MOUNTAIN MIDDLE SCHOOL
Furnace Woods Road
Peekskill, NY 10566

BLUE SPRINGS HIGH SCHOOL
2000 West Ashton Dr.
Blue Springs, MO 64015

BOOKER T. WASHINGTON SENIOR HIGH SCHOOL*
1631 E. Woodrow Place
Tulsa, OK 74106

BOUNTIFUL HIGH SCHOOL
695 South Orchard Dr.
Bountiful, UT 84010

BRANDON HIGH SCHOOL*
1101 Victoria St.
Brandon, FL 33511

BRANDYWINE HIGH SCHOOL*
1400 Foulk Road
Wilmington, DE 19803

BRIDGE STREET JUNIOR HIGH SCHOOL
Bridge Street Junior Ave.
Wheeling, WV 26003

BRIGHTON HIGH SCHOOL
2220 East 7600 South
Salt Lake City, UT 84121

*participating schools

BRONX HIGH SCHOOL OF SCIENCE
75 West 205th St.
Bronx, NY 10468

BROOKLAND JUNIOR HIGH SCHOOL
Michigan Ave. and Randolph,
NE, Washington, DC 20017

BROOKLYN TECHNICAL HIGH
SCHOOL
29 Fort Green Pl.
Brooklyn, NY 11217

BUTLER MIDDLE SCHOOL*
7530 South 2700 East
Salt Lake City, UT 84121

CALAPOOIA MIDDLE SCHOOL*
830 East 24th
Albany, OR 97321-4299

CAMDEN HIGH SCHOOL
Laurens St.
Camden, SC 29020

CAPTAIN SHREVE HIGH SCHOOL*
6115 East Kings Highway
Shreveport, LA 71105

CARMEL HIGH SCHOOL*
520 East Main St.
Carmel, IN 46032

CARMODY JUNIOR HIGH SCHOOL
2050 S. Kipling St.
Lakewood, CO 80227

CASHMERE MIDDLE SCHOOL
Tigner Road
Cashmere, WA 98815

CAVE SPRINGS HIGH SCHOOL
3712 Chaparrell Dr., SW
Roanoke, VA 24018

CEDAR PARK INTERMEDIATE SCHOOL
P.O. Box 200
Beaverton, OR 97075

CENTRAL JUNIOR HIGH SCHOOL
515 Clark St.
Ames, IA 50010

CHANDLER HIGH SCHOOL*
350 North Arizona Ave.
Chandler, AZ 85224

CHEYENNE MOUNTAIN
HIGH SCHOOL*
1200 Cresta Road
Colorado Springs, CO 80906

CLAY JUNIOR HIGH SCHOOL*
5150 E. 126th St.
Carmel, IN 46032

CLEVELAND HIGH SCHOOL
850 Raider Dr.
Cleveland, TN 37311

CLINTON HIGH SCHOOL*
711 Lakeview
Clinton, MS 39056

COLLIERVILLE MIDDLE SCHOOL*
1101 North Byhalia Road
Collierville, TN 38017

CRATER HIGH SCHOOL
4410 N. Rogue Valley Blvd.
Central Point, OR 97502

CURTIS HIGH SCHOOL
8425 West 40th St.
Tacoma, WA 98466

DARREL C. SWOPE MIDDLE SCHOOL
901 Keele Dr.
Reno, NV 98103

DAVIDSON MIDDLE SCHOOL*
280 Woodland Ave.
San Rafael, CA 94901

DEERING HIGH SCHOOL
370 Stevens Ave.
Portland, ME 04103

DOUGLAS MIDDLE SCHOOL*
7th and Walnut, Box 1028
Douglas, WY 82633

DOUGLAS MCARTHUR
MIDDLE SCHOOL
1615 Wilkins
Jonesboro, AR 72401

E.C. GLASS HIGH SCHOOL
2111 Memorial Ave.
Lynchburg, VA 24501

EASTVIEW MIDDLE SCHOOL
3195 Spring Valley Road
Bath, OH 44210

ELKO HIGH SCHOOL
987 College Ave.
Elko, NV 89801

ELM PLACE MIDDLE SCHOOL
2031 Sheridan Road
Highland Park, IL 60035

GEORGE V. LEY VA
INTERMEDIATE SCHOOL*
1865 Monrovia Dr.
San Jose, CA 95148

GEORGE MASON JUNIOR-SENIOR
HIGH SCHOOL
1724 Leesburg Pike
Falls Church, VA 22046

GRACE KING HIGH SCHOOL
4301 Grace King Pl.
Metairie, LA 70002

GROSSE POINTE SOUTH
HIGH SCHOOL
11 Grosse Point Blvd.
Grosse Point, MI 48236

HANFORD SECONDARY SCHOOL
450 Hanford St.
Richland, WA 99352

HANOVER HIGH SCHOOL*
Lebanon St.
Hanover, NH 03755

HAZEN PUBLIC HIGH SCHOOL*
520 1st Ave., NE
Hazen, ND 58545

HIGHLAND HIGH SCHOOL*
2166 South 17th East
Salt Lake City, UT 84106

HOMEWOOD-FLOSSMOOR
HIGH SCHOOL
999 Kedzie Ave.
Flossmoor, IL 60422

HOOVER MIDDLE SCHOOL*
12015 Tivoli, NE
Albuquerque, NM 87111

HOPKINS HIGH SCHOOL
2400 Lindbergh Dr.
Minnetonka, MN 55343

HUGH BAIN JUNIOR HIGH SCHOOL
135 Gansett Ave.
Cranston, RI 02910

ILLING JUNIOR HIGH SCHOOL*
227 East Middle Turnpike
Manchester, CT 06040

INDIAN HILLS JUNIOR
HIGH SCHOOL*
9401 Indian Hills Dr.
Des Moines, IA 50322

IRMO HIGH SCHOOL*
6671 Saint Andrews Road
Columbia, SC 29210

JAMES LOGAN HIGH SCHOOL
1800 H St.
Union City, CA 94587

JEFFERSON JUNIOR HIGH SCHOOL*
8th and H Streets, SW
Washington, DC 20024

JEFFERSON DAVIS JUNIOR
HIGH SCHOOL*
7050 Melvin Road
Jacksonville, FL 32210

JOHN ADAMS JUNIOR HIGH SCHOOL
1525 NW 31st St.
Rochester, MN 55901

JOHN J. RHODES JUNIOR
HIGH SCHOOL*
1860 South Longmore Road
Mesa, AZ 85202

JOHN MARSHALL HIGH SCHOOL*
9017 N. University
Oklahoma City, OK 73114

JONESBORO HIGH SCHOOL*
301 Hurricane Dr.
Jonesboro, AR 72401

KATAHDIN HIGH SCHOOL*
Sherman Station
Sherman Mills, ME 04777

KEARNEY JUNIOR HIGH SCHOOL*
915 W. 35th St.
Kearney, NE 68847

KEOKUK MIDDLE SCHOOL
14th and Main
Keokuk, IA 52632

KENNEBUNK HIGH SCHOOL*
Fletcher St.
Kennebunk, ME 04043

KENNY C. GUINN JUNIOR
HIGH SCHOOL
4150 South Torrey Pine
Las Vegas, NV 89103

KICKAPOO HIGH SCHOOL*
3710 S. Jefferson
Springfield, MO 65807

KING MIDDLE SCHOOL
92 Deering Ave.
Portland, ME 04102

LADUE HORTON WATKINS
HIGH SCHOOL
1201 South Warson Dr.
St. Louis, MO 63124

LAKE OSWEGO HIGH SCHOOL*
2501 SW Country Club Road
Lake Oswego, OR 97034

LAKEWOOD JUNIOR HIGH SCHOOL
124 E. 3rd St.
Luling, LA 70080

LEAGUE MIDDLE SCHOOL*
125 Twin Lake Road
Greenville, SC 29609

LEBANON JUNIOR HIGH SCHOOL
75 Bank St.
Lebanon, NH 03766

LEE COUNTY SENIOR HIGH SCHOOL*
1708 Nash St.
Sanford, NC 27330

LEESVILLE HIGH SCHOOL*
502 Berry Ave.
Leesville, LA 71446

LINCOLN HIGH SCHOOL
Old River Road
Lincoln, RI 02865

LOGAN SENIOR HIGH SCHOOL
162 West First South
Logan, UT 84321

LOUIS ARMSTRONG MIDDLE SCHOOL*
32-02 Junction Blvd.
East Elmhurst, NY 11369

LOWELL HIGH SCHOOL
1101 Eucalyptus Dr.
San Francisco, CA 94132

MANZANO HIGH SCHOOL*
12200 Lomas Blvd.
Albuquerque, NM 87112

McCOMB HIGH SCHOOL*
310 7th St.
McComb, MS 39648

MEAD JUNIOR HIGH SCHOOL
North 12509 Market St.
Mead, WA 99021

MEMORIAL HIGH SCHOOL
225 Keith St.
Eau Claire, WI 54701

MIDDLEBROOK HIGH SCHOOL*
363 Danbury Road
Wilton, CT 06897

MILLARD SOUTH HIGH SCHOOL
14905 Q St.
Omaha, NE 68137

MRACHEK MIDDLE SCHOOL
1955 S. Telluride
Aurora, CO 80013

MOUNT ARARAT SCHOOL*
Mount Ararat Topsham,
MSAD 75
Topsham, ME 04086

NISKAYUNA HIGH SCHOOL
1626 Balltown Road
Schenectady, NY 12309

NORTH CENTRAL HIGH SCHOOL*
1801 East 86th St.
Indianapolis, IN 46240

OAKLEA MIDDLE SCHOOL*
1515 Rose St.
Junction City, OR 97448

PARKWAY WEST SENIOR
HIGH SCHOOL*
75 Clayton Road
Ballwin, MO 63011

PASCO SENIOR HIGH SCHOOL
10th & West Henry Streets
Pasco, WA 99301

PERKINS JUNIOR HIGH SCHOOL
630 Mull Ave.
Akron, OH 44313

PINE BLUFFS HIGH SCHOOL
7th & Elm Streets
Pine Bluffs, WY 82082

PIONEER HIGH SCHOOL*
10800 Benavon St.
Whittier, CA 90606

PRINCETON JUNIOR HIGH SCHOOL
11080 Chester Road
Cincinnati, OH 45246

PROSPECT HEIGHTS
MIDDLE SCHOOL*
200 Caroline St.
Orange, VA 22960

RACELAND JUNIOR HIGH SCHOOL*
PO Box C
Raceland, LA 70394

RENNE INTERMEDIATE SCHOOL
620 E. 6th St.
Newburg, OR 97132

RIBAULT HIGH SCHOOL
3701 Winton Dr.
Jacksonville, FL 32208

ROSCOMMON HIGH SCHOOL
10600 Oakwood Road
Roscommon, MI 48653

RUFUS KING HIGH SCHOOL
1801 West Olive St.
Milwaukee, WI 53209

SACAJAWEA JUNIOR HIGH SCHOOL*
East 401 33rd Ave.
Spokane, WA 99203

SCARSDALE HIGH SCHOOL
Post Road
Scarsdale, NY 10583

SHAKER HEIGHTS HIGH SCHOOL*
15911 Aldersyde Dr.
Shaker Heights, OH 44120

SHOREHAM-WADING RIVER
MIDDLE SCHOOL
Randall Road
Shoreham, NY 11786

SHOREWOOD HIGH SCHOOL*
17300 Fremont Ave. North
Seattle, WA 98133

SHUE MIDDLE SCHOOL
1500 Capitol Trail
Newark, DE 19711

SIMON PERKINS MIDDLE SCHOOL*
630 Mull Ave.
Akron, OH 44313

SNOWDEN SCHOOL
1870 North Pkwy.
Memphis, TN 38112

SOLDOTNA JUNIOR HIGH SCHOOL*
PO Box 1070
Soldotna, AK 99669

SOLDOTNA HIGH SCHOOL
PO Box 3009
Soldotna, AK 99669

SOUTH EAST JUNIOR HIGH SCHOOL*
2501 Bradford Dr.
Iowa City, IA 52240

SOUTH EUGENE HIGH SCHOOL
400 East 19th Ave.
Eugene, OR 97401

SOUTH PLANTATION HIGH SCHOOL*
1300 SW 54th Ave.
Plantation, FL 33317

SOUTHSIDE HIGH SCHOOL
4100 Gary St.
Fort Smith, AR 72903

SPARTANBURG SENIOR
HIGH SCHOOL*
Dupre Dr.
Spartanburg, SC 29302

SPRING VALLEY HIGH SCHOOL*
Sparkleberry Lane
Columbia, SC 29206

STEPHEN F. AUSTIN HIGH SCHOOL*
1715 West First St.
Austin, TX 78703

STURGIS PUBLIC HIGH SCHOOL
216 Vinewood
Sturgis, MI 49091

STUYVESANT HIGH SCHOOL*
345 East 15th St.
New York, NY 10003

SUNSET HIGH SCHOOL
PO Box 200
Beaverton, OR 97075

T.C. WILLIAMS HIGH SCHOOL
3330 King St.
Alexandria, VA 22302

TAFT MIDDLE SCHOOL*
620 Schulte Road, NW
Albuquerque, NM 87107

TERRACE HILLS JUNIOR
HIGH SCHOOL*
22579 DeBerry
Grand Terrace, CA 92324

TRIADELPHIA JUNIOR HIGH SCHOOL
1636 National Road
Wheeling, WV 26003

VALDEZ HIGH SCHOOL*
Box 398
Valdez, AK 99686

VALPARAISO HIGH SCHOOL*
2727 N. Campbell St.
Valparaiso, IN 46383

VENADO MIDDLE SCHOOL
4 Deerfield Ave.
Irvine, CA 92714

WARREN CENTRAL HIGH SCHOOL*
9500 East 16th St.
Indianapolis, IN 46229

WASATCH MIDDLE SCHOOL*
200 East 800 South
Heber City, UT 84032

WEBSTER TRANSITIONAL SCHOOL*
W75 N624 Wauwatosa Road
Cedarburg, WI 53012

WELCH JUNIOR HIGH SCHOOL
321 State St.
Ames, IA 50010

WEST OTTAWA MIDDLE SCHOOL
3700 140th Ave.
Holland, MI 49423

WESTCHESTER MIDDLE SCHOOL*
1050 S. 5th St.
Chesterton, IN 46304

WHEELING JUNIOR HIGH SCHOOL
3500 Chapline St.
Wheeling, WV 26003

WILLIAM A. CROCKER JUNIOR
HIGH SCHOOL
2600 Ralston Ave.
Hillsborough, CA 94010

WILLIAM G. ENLOE HIGH SCHOOL
128 Clarendon Crescent
Raleigh, NC 27610

WILLIS JUNIOR HIGH SCHOOL
401 South McQueen Road
Chandler, AZ 85202

WILTON HIGH SCHOOL
395 Danbury Road
Wilton, CT 06897

WINSTON CHURCHILL HIGH SCHOOL*
12049 Blanco Road
San Antonio, TX 78216

WOOSTER INTERMEDIATE SCHOOL*
150 Lincoln St.
Stratford, CT 06497

WYOMING HIGH SCHOOL*
106 Pendery Ave.
Wyoming, OH 45215

YORK COMMUNITY HIGH SCHOOL
355 W. Saint Charles Road
Elmhurst, IL 60126

PRINCIPALS PARTICIPATING IN THE UNIVERSITY OF TEXAS AT AUSTIN STUDY OF TEACHING EXCELLENCE

GEORGE J. BELLO
Albuquerque High School
Albuquerque, NM

ELMO E. BROUSSARD
Raceland Junior High School
Raceland, LA

LINDA W. BROWN
South Plantation High School
Plantation, FL

ELTON CHURCHILL
Winston Churchill High School
San Antonio, TX

LORETTA COLLIER
Booker T. Washington Senior
High School
Tulsa, OK

HOWARD K. CONLEY
Chandler High School
Chandler, AZ

ALFRED DEL HERMAN
Louis Armstrong Middle School
East Elmhurst, NY

JOSEPH D. DELANEY
Spartanburg High School
Spartanburg, SC

DON K. DELLER
Westchester Middle School
Chesterton, IN

C. WILLIAM DUDLEY
Wasatch Middle School
Heber City, UT

LEON EDD
John Marshall High School
Oklahoma City, OK

JOHN FINK
Wyoming High School
Wyoming, OH

DELBERT H. FOWLER
Highland High School
Salt Lake City, UT

JOHN GARRISON
Hoover Middle School
Albuquerque, NM

DALE E. GRAHAM
Carmel High School
Carmel, IN

GEORGE E. HAMES
Wooster Intermediate School
Stratford, CT

W. TERRENCE HANNON
Taft Middle School
Albuquerque, NM

ELDON K. HELM
Cheyenne Mountain
High School
Colorado Springs, CO

JO ANN KRUEGER
Manzano High School
Albuquerque, NM

RICHARD F. LINDGREN
Illing Junior High School
Manchester, CT

SANDRA McCALLA
Captain Shreve High School
Shreveport, LA

MAJOR V. McCARTY
Irmo High School
Columbia, SC

JACQUELYN McGEE
Stephen F. Austin High School
Austin, TX

ERNEST MEDCALFE
Warren Central High School
Indianapolis, IN

GERALD MENKE
Kearney Junior High School
Kearney, NE

ARTHUR O. MOTZ
Soldotna Junior High School
Soldotna, AK

WILLIAM BEN NESBIT
Spring Valley High School
Columbia, SC

PAUL NYS
Calapooia Middle School
Albany, OR

MORRIS H. PIXLEY
Sacajawea Junior High School
Spokane, WA

WAYNE H. PORTER
Douglas Middle School
Douglas, WY

RICHARD REESE
Leesville High School
Leesville, LA

LOREN RITCHIE
Katahdin High School
Sherman Mills, ME

GEORGE W. SEAGRAVES
Lee County Senior High School
Sanford, NC

ROBERT L. THEIL
Clay Junior High School
Carmel, IN

DAN E. YOUNG
John J. Rhodes Junior
High School
Mesa, AZ

C. A. ZIMMERMAN
Shaker Heights High School
Shaker Heights, OH

TEACHERS PARTICIPATING IN THE UNIVERSITY OF TEXAS AT AUSTIN STUDY OF TEACHING EXCELLENCE

JAYNEEN AKINS
Business
Annie Camp Middle School
Jonesboro, AR

DIANA LYNNE ANDERSON
Art
Spring Valley High School
Columbia, SC

DAVID T. ARNOLD
Social Studies
Clay Junior High School
Carmel, IN

DAVID BARDOS
Social Studies
Carmel High School
Carmel, IN

BRENDA BARRE
Social Studies
Booker T. Washington Senior
High School
Tulsa, OK

FRANCES BATES
Vocal Music
Kearney Junior High School
Kearney, NE

RAE M. BATES
English
Katahdin High School
Sherman Mills, ME

BARBARA BELLUOMINI
English
Davidson Middle School
San Rafael, CA

PAUL J. BENZ
Mathematics
Clay Junior High School
Carmel, IN

LINDA BERGLAND
Mathematics
Hazen High School
Hazen, ND

DONNA LYNNE BOGLE
Special Education
Stephen F. Austin High School
Austin, TX

VICTORIA BROCK
Media Specialist
Westchester Middle School
Chesterton, IN

FRANCES M. BURGESS
Business
Jonesboro High School
Jonesboro, AR

FRANCES A. CARNEY
Counseling
John J. Rhodes Junior
High School
Mesa, AZ

CHESTER CHASE
Mathematics
Katahdin High School
Sherman Mills, ME

HENRIETTA CAVANAUGH
Mathematics
Leesville High School
Leesville, LA

SHERI CHILDS
English
Captain Shreve High School
Shreveport, LA

SANDRA S. CLINGER
Mathematics
Brandon High School
Brandon, FL

JUDITH LYNNE COLE
Social Studies
Manzano High School
Albuquerque, NM

NANCY R. COPE
Social Studies
Lee County Senior High School
Sanford, NC

DOROTHY M. CORD
English
Clay Junior High School
Carmel, IN

DEBORAH CHERYL COURTER
6th Grade
Prospect Heights Middle School
Orange, VA

ALICE S. CULPEPPER
English
South Plantation High School
Plantation, FL

ADELAIDE DE MEDEIROS
Social Studies
George V. Ley Va
Intermediate School
San Jose, CA

SHARON DEAL
Science
Spring Valley High School
Columbia, SC

RICHARD M. DELL'ERGO
Social Studies
John J. Rhodes Junior
High School
Mesa, AZ

DR. JOHN Y. DEMPSEY
Science
Leesville High School
Leesville, LA

BARBARA W. DILLEY
Mathematics
Soldotna Junior High School
Soldotna, AK

MINA DOSHER
Special Education
Hoover Middle School
Albuquerque, NM

PAUL DYKES
English
Booker T. Washington
Senior High School
Tulsa, OK

SUSAN EIDE
Business
Valdez High School
Valdez, AK

MARGIE K. EUSTICE
Social Studies
Simon Perkins Middle School
Akron, OH

ELIZABETH FALGOUT
English
Raceland Junior High School
Raceland, LA

PHILIP FAULKNER
Physical Education
Katahdin High School
Sherman Mills, ME

P. MARYETTA FERRE
Reading
Terrace Hills Junior
High School
Grand Terrace, CA

JOHN FIGORAS
Industrial Arts
Wooster Intermediate School
Stratford, CT

DONNA M. FITZGERALD
Art
Illing Junior High School
Manchester, CT

CHARLES P. FITZSIMMONS
Science
Simon Perkins Middle School
Akron, OH

LEVI CLAYTON FOLLY
English
Prospect Heights Middle School
Orange, VA

RICHARD GARRETT
Social Studies
John Marshall High School
Oklahoma City, OK

ARTHUR I. GLAZE, JR.
Spanish
Winston Churchill High School
San Antonio, TX

CYNTHIA H. GODFREY
English
Spartanburg High School
Spartanburg, SC

WILLIAM M. GOULDY
French
John Marshall High School
Oklahoma City, OK

MAGGIE DIXON GREEN
Remedial Reading
Captain Shreve High School
Shreveport, LA

NANCY BRAZIER GREEN
Spanish/French
Booker T. Washington
Senior High School
Tulsa, OK

TRESA TAYLOR HADNOT
English
Leesville High School
Leesville, LA

SUSAN HARDING
Spanish
John Marshall High School
Oklahoma City, OK

RONALD D. HELLEMS
Vocal Music
Carmel High School
Carmel, IN

ANNA HICKS
English
Irmo High School
Columbia, SC

KAREN M. HIGGINS
Mathematics
Oaklea Middle School
Junction City, OR

WILLIAM D. HULLING
Social Studies
Indian Hills Junior High School
Des Moines, IA

ULYSSES JACKSON
Science
South Plantation High School
Plantation, FL

STEVEN K. JANECKY
Special Education
Manzano High School
Albuquerque, NM

BRENDAN KENNY
English
Stephen F. Austin High School
Austin, TX

THOMAS A. KESSINGER
Social Studies
Wyoming High School
Wyoming, OH

SANDRA KEY
English
Jonesboro High School
Jonesboro, AR

WILLIAM F. KOLTER
Vocational Education
Chandler High School
Chandler, AZ

DALE KRUEGER
Mathematics
Irmo High School
Columbia, SC

MICHAEL LAFORGIA
Social Studies
Louis Armstrong Middle School
East Elmhurst, NY

ANNE LEEPANSEN
Special Education
Valdez High School
Valdez, AK

HAL W. LINDFELT
Social Studies
Cheyenne Mountain
High School
Colorado Springs, CO

CAROL LOVATO
History
Albuquerque High School
Albuquerque, NM

DR. LAURIE ANDREW LYON
Science
Lee County Senior High School
Sanford, NC

WESLEY W. MAIERS
Mathematics
Valparaiso High School
Valparaiso, IN

MICHAEL J. MARQUIS
English
Illing Junior High School
Manchester, CT

LAWRENCE M. MARRS
General Subjects
Oaklea Middle School
Junction City, OR

MARKY S. MAUGHAN
English
Soldotna Junior High School
Soldotna, AK

ROBERT B. MAXWELL
English
Raceland Junior High School
Raceland, LA

MARCIA J. MENDENHALL
English
Indian Hills Junior High School
Des Moines, IA

LINDA SUE MERCER
English
Jefferson Davis Junior
High School
Jacksonville, FL

GEORGE MILLAY
Mathematics
Mount Ararat School
Topsham, ME

CONNIE S. MILLER
Home Economics
Spring Valley High School
Columbia, SC

ANGIE MITCHELL
English
Westchester Middle School
Chesterton, IN

MAXINE H. MOORE
Science
Spartanburg High School
Spartanburg, SC

CAROLYN ELIZABETH NASH
Business
Prospect Heights Middle School
Orange, VA

RUTH ANNE NICHOLSON
Spanish
Irmo High School
Columbia, SC

GAIL OLIVER
Reading
Taft Middle School
Albuquerque, NM

BRIGITTE H. O'MALLEY
Business
Taft Middle School
Albuquerque, NM

L. D. NAEGELIN
English
Winston Churchill High School
San Antonio, TX

CHERYL OTIS NICOLA
English
Hazen High School
Hazen, ND

ANDRA ONCALE
Special Education
Raceland Junior High School
Raceland, LA

JAMES R. OWENS
Mathematics
Albuquerque High School
Albuquerque, NM

GERALD R. PAGE
Mathematics
Indian Hills Junior High School
Des Moines, IA

HAROLD D. PETERSEN
Art
Highland High School
Salt Lake City, UT

HAROLD PIATT
Mathematics
Manzano High School
Albuquerque, NM

PATRICK N. POPE
Computer Science
Jefferson Junior High School
Washington, DC

FRANCES M. RACINE
Social Science
Spartanburg High School
Spartanburg, SC

ANGELA M. RAMIREZ
English
Taft Middle School
Albuquerque, NM

MARJORIE RATLIFF
Science
Lake Oswego High School
Lake Oswego, OR

DON RIBBING
English
Parkway West High School
Ballwin, MO

LINDA ROTTMAN
Physical Education
John J. Rhodes Junior
High School
Mesa, AZ

HUGH D. RUSH
English
Highland High School
Salt Lake City, UT

THOMAS RUSSO
English
Illing Junior High School
Manchester, CT

STACEY SAVAGE-BROOKS
Art
Louis Armstrong Middle School
East Elmhurst, NY

BRIAN W. SCHENK
Social Studies
Stephen F. Austin High School
Austin, TX

TOM SHIELD
Mathematics
Kearney Junior High School
Kearney, NE

MARK SHOUP
English
Carmel High School
Carmel, IN

LYNN D. SIMPSON
Spanish
Annie Camp Middle School
Jonesboro, AR

JEAN STEVENS
Music
Davidson Middle School
San Rafael, CA

STEWART R. STILKEY
Science
Mount Ararat School
Topsham, ME

JOHN STRANG
Mathematics
Valdez High School
Valdez, AK

MARILYN SULLIVAN
Drama
Hoover Middle School
Albuquerque, NM

MARCIA SWANSON
Mathematics
Calapooia Middle School
Albany, OR

KAY MAUREEN SWEDBERG
English
Albuquerque High School
Albuquerque, NM

DORANE TEAGUE
Science
Hoover Middle School
Albuquerque, NM

VICKIE TODD
Special Education
Wasatch Middle School
Heber City, UT

PAUL G. TROJAK
Social Studies
Brandon High School
Brandon, FL

FRANCES MINKINS TUCKER
Science
Chandler High School
Chandler, AZ

JENNE LEE TWIFORD
English
Douglas Middle School
Douglas, WY

EDWARD WALFORD
Chemistry
Cheyenne Mountain
High School
Colorado Springs, CO

LARRY K. WARD
Science
Wasatch Middle School
Heber City, UT

CHARLES J. WEST
English
Kearney Junior High School
Kearney, NE

Jo Amy Wynn
Mathematics
Captain Shreve High School
Shreveport, LA

Alison Youkilis
Art
Wyoming High School
Wyoming, OH

Lavon Young
Physical Education
McComb High School
McComb, MS

Ann Marie Zdanowicz
Home Economics
Mount Ararat School
Topsham, ME

DESCRIPTION OF THE STUDY

I n 1982, while numerous commissions and boards were studying how American education should be improved, Peters and Waterman produced a bestseller describing excellent American companies, *In Search of Excellence*. Our analysis of their study convinced us that their eight basic findings also applied to education in general. We felt that each of the eight qualities found in exceptional companies expressed generic organizational and leadership characteristics that could be translated easily into educational terms. The Peters and Waterman attribute, "close to the customer," clearly translates "close to the student." Similarly, "productivity through people" relates to "student achievement and satisfaction through schooling"with the help of those professionals who work in schools.

We strongly believe that one does not build an excellent school solely by upgrading the design and delivery of instruction. Such efforts may indeed provide a better vehicle, but we believe that little lasting improvement will occur without a focus and a commitment to excellence through the performance of the human beings within the school.

To test the efficacy of our ideas, we selected for study the 154 secondary schools selected as the best in America (in 1982) by the Department of Education's Secondary School Recognition Program (SSRP). With 50 states and the District of Columbia participating, the SSRP selected the best 154 schools from the 396 nominated. Based on the assumption that in order to discover what makes excellence, excellent institutions and performers must be studied, we focused our investigation on the school climates, teachers, and principals of the 154 outstanding schools. Guiding our study were these main purposes:

1. To improve teaching in American schools
2. To improve school leadership
3. To attract able teachers and leaders into education
4. To develop models of excellence in teaching and school leadership
5. To identify and reward excellence already present among our nation's secondary schools.

Consequently, our approach was to discern excellence through careful scrutiny of the actions and rationales of outstanding teachers and principals in secondary schools recognized by the SSRP. While recognizing that the Department of Education program represents but one means of selecting outstanding schools and that their list does not begin to include all exemplary schools, we nevertheless decided on their list of schools for our sample because we agree with the criteria that were used in selecting the schools. Those criteria are enumerated in the preface of this volume. Furthermore, given time and resource constraints, conducting our own selection process was not entirely justified when a list of excellent schools was already available from the Education Department's Secondary School Recognition Program.

The 154 schools were selected by the Department of Education according to 14 criteria of excellent qualities of effective schools. Outside site evaluation teams visited each of the 154 schools and assessed the validity of these criteria as part of the SSRP conditions for selection. We decided also to assess the qualities of the principals participating in our study against the eight Peters and Waterman leadership attributes. Finally, we selected 12 teaching themes developed by Selection Research, Inc. (SRI), Lincoln, Nebraska, as those qualities to study in the participating teachers. As with all qualitative research endeavors, hypotheses changed as we proceeded with the investigation. The characteristics against which we measured the qualities of excellent teachers and principals became more accurately defined and modified as the study progressed.

The Research Design

We designed and developed two instruments for measuring the extent to which principals were characterized by the eight Peters and Waterman leader attributes. We asked principals to evaluate themselves against these qualities and to further nominate and evaluate three excellent teachers who met the 12 SRI teaching criteria. We then developed two additional instruments to determine the extent to which the nominated exceptional teachers were characterized by the attributes outlined in the 12 Selection Research teaching themes. Teachers were asked to evaluate themselves against the SRI teaching themes and to further evaluate the principal against the eight Peters and Waterman attributes.

We wanted to study schools with extraordinary commitment to excellence and where principals and teachers were motivated to commit to the onerous process of completing our survey instruments because they believed that their schools were extraordinary and that their stories deserved to be told. We wanted to study the best of the best and surmised that only the most dedicated and committed would agree to spend the time necessary to participate in our study. In the final sample of the secondary schools, we examined and analyzed 39 exceptional school climates, 34 exceptional principals, and 89 exceptional secondary teachers.

Assumptions

Research into successful organizations has been revitalized and revamped by the highly successful Peters and Waterman study. In spite of criticism from traditional researchers, this work best epitomizes John Gardner's dream of striving for the highest standards, identifying appropriate effort and performance, and demanding quality for ourselves and for our fellows.

In their model, Peters and Waterman provided us with the key assumption upon which our research would rest. That is, the dominant influence on quality and excellence in institutions is attention to people, not attention to work conditions. Linking Peters and Waterman's concepts to the selection criteria established by the Department of Education's Secondary School Recognition Program was done without difficulty.

The other major assumption on which our study is founded is that the Behavioral Event Interview Technique (BEIT), conceived by Harvard psychologist David McClelland, is an effective research tool for discerning competencies that lead to effective performance. The BEIT is a type of content analysis we used to delineate patterns recurring among the narrative responses of the subjects in our study. Since the teachers and principals participating in our study responded to questions specificially designed to elicit values, attitudes, and rationales for actions, the technique tends to tap antecedents to behaviors that are not apparent through direct observation. Thus, by employing this methodology, we have not only analyzed the behaviors of effective performers but have also analyzed the reasons and motivations behind those behaviors. The technique is an attempt to objectify and empiricize the study of human behavior, to the degree that is possible, for the purpose of discovering knowledge about human beings in order to help others develop qualities that appear to result in effective performance among successful individuals.

REFERENCES

Achilles, C.M., and Keedy, J.L. "Principal Norm Setting as a Component of Effective Schools." *National Forum of Educational Administration and Supervision* 1, 1 (1983-84): 58-68.

Adelman, C., et al. (1983, March). "Devaluation, Diffusion, and the College Connection: A Study of High School Transcripts, 1964-1981." Prepared for the National Commission on Excellence. Quoted in Ernest L. Boyer, *High School: A Report of the Carnegie Foundation for the Advancement of Teaching.* New York: Harper & Row, 1983.

Adler, M.J. *The Paideia Problems and Possibilities.* New York: MacMillan, 1983.

Albrecht, J.E. "A Nation at Risk: Another View." *Phi Delta Kappan* 65, 10 (1984): 684.

Albrecht, J.E., and Duea, J. "What Price Excellence?: The Iowa Experience." *Phi Delta Kappan* 65, 3 (1983): 211-213.

Allen, R.R. "On the Nature of Teaching Excellence." *Journal of the Wisconsin Communication Association* 3 (1983): 1-5.

Armor, D., et al. *Analysis of the School Preferred Reading Program in Selected Los Angeles Schools.* Prepared for the Los Angeles Unified School District. Santa Monica, Calif.: Rand Corp., 1976.

Aspy, D. "A Discussion of the Relationship between Selected Student Behavior and the Teacher's Use of Interchangeable Responses." Paper presented at American Educational Research Association, New Orleans, La., 1973.

Aspy, D., and Roebuck, F. "From Humane Ideas to Human Technology and Back Again Many Times." *Education* 95 (Winter 1974): 63-172.

Austin, G.R. "Exemplary Schools and the Search for Effectiveness." *Educational Record* 37 (1979): 10-14.

Baker, G.A.; Boggs, G.R.; and Putman, S. "Ideal Environment Nurtures Excellence." *Community and Junior College Journal* 54, 2 (1983): 26-29.

Barr, R., and Dreeben, R. "Instruction in Teaching." In *Review of Research in Education,* pp. 89-162. Edited by L.S. Shulman. Itasca, Il.: F.E. Peacock Publishers, Inc., and the Association for Supervision and Curriculum Development, 1977.

Bell, T.H. *Meeting the Challenge: Recent Efforts to Improve Education Across the Nation.* Washington, D.C.: U.S. Department of Education, 1983.

Benbow, C. *Review of Instructionally Effective Schooling Literature.* ERIC/CUE No. 70. (ERIC Document Reproduction Service No. ED 194 682), 1980.

Benjamin, R. *Making Schools Work.* New York: Continuum, 1981.

Bennett, N. *Teaching Styles and Pupil Progress.* Cambridge: Harvard University Press, 1976.

Berliner, D.C. "Tempus Educare." In *Research on Teaching: Concepts, Findings and Implications,* pp. 120-135. Edited by P. Peterson and H.J. Walberg. Berkeley: McCutchan, 1979.

Berliner, D. "The Executive Functions of Teaching." Paper presented at the meeting of the Wingspread Conference on relating to Classroom Instruction, Racine, Wis., and the American Educational Research Association meeting, New York, March 1982.

Billups, L.H., and Rauth, M. "The New Research: How Effective Teachers Teach." *American Educator* 8 (1984): 34-39.

Blai, B., Jr. *Effective College Teaching Facilitates Student Thinking at a Junior College.* (ERIC Document Reproduction Service No. ED 182 713), 1982.

Block, R. "We Already Know Our Problems Out Here in the Field." *Phi Delta Kappan* 65, 3 (1983): 183.

Bloom, B. *Human Characteristics and School Learning.* New York: McGraw-Hill, 1976.

Blumberg, A., and Greenfield, W. *The Effective Principal: Perspectives on School Leadership.* Boston: Allyn and Bacon, Inc., 1980.

Borho, H.; Cone, R.; Russo, N.A.; and Shavelson, R.J. "Teachers' Decision-Making." In *Research on Teaching: Concepts, Findings, and Implications,* pp. 136-159. Edited by P. Peterson and H.J. Walberg. Berkeley, Calif.: McCutchan, 1979.

Boyer, E. *High School: A Report of the Carnegie Foundation for the Advancement of Teaching.* New York: Harper and Row, 1983.

Bracey, G.W. "On the Compelling Need to Go Beyond Minimum Competency." *Phi Delta Kappan* 64, 10 (1983): 717-721.

Brookover, W.B., and Lezotte, L.W. *Changes in School Characteristics Coincident with Changes in Student Achievement.* Occasional Paper No. 17. East Lansing, Mich.: Institute for Research on Teaching, Michigan State University, May 1979.

Brophy, J.E. "Teacher Behavior and Student Learning." *Educational Leadership* 37, 1 (1979): 33-38.

Brophy, J.E. "Teacher Praise: A Functional Analysis." *Psychological Review* 88, 2 (Spring 1981): 93-134.

Brophy, J.E. "Classroom Management and Learning." *American Education* 18, 2 (1982): 20-23.

Brophy, J.E., and Good, T.L. *Teacher-Student Relationships.* New York: Holt, Rinehart and Winston, Inc., 1974.

Brown-Richau, L. "U.S. Education Reaches Crisis Stage; Texas Hopes to Increase Basic Skills." *The Daily Texan,* May 4, (1983): 1.

Brundage, Diane, ed. *What Makes an Effective School?* Studies of schools that work in Arkansas, Florida, Maine, Maryland, Nebraska, Virginia, Urban District M4 Nationwide. The Journalism Research Fellows Report. Washington, D.C.: Institute for Educational Leadership, George Washington University, 1980.

Bureau of School Programs Evaluation. *Three Strategies for Studying the Effects of School Processes: An Expanded Edition of Which School Factors Relate to Learning.* Albany, N.Y.: New York State Education Department, University of the State of New York, March 1976.

Caldwell, W.E., and Lutz, F.W. "The Measurement of Principal Rule Administration Behavior and Its Relationship to Educational Leadership." *Educational Leadership Quarterly* 14, 2 (1978): 63-79.

Cawelti, G. "Behavior Patterns of Effective Principals." *Educational Leadership* 41, 5 (1984): 3.

Center of Educational Research and Development. *Process Evaluation: A Comprehensive Study of Outliers.* Baltimore, Md.: Maryland State Department of Education, University of Maryland, February 1978.

Center on Evaluation, Development, and Research. "The Changing Role of the Principal." Selections from a CEDR Seminar held at Phi Delta Kappa International Headquarters, December 1, 1983. In *The Role of the Principal,* pp. 5-12. Hot Topics Series, No. 1. Bloomington, Ind.: Phi Delta Kappa, 1984.

Centra, J.A., and Potter, D.A. "School and Teacher Effects: An Interrelational Model." *Review of Educational Research* 50 (Summer 1980): 273-291.

Chandler, H.N. "Just Among Us Teachers." *Phi Delta Kappan* 65, 3 (1983): 178-180.

Clark, D.L., and Lotto, L.S. "Principals in Instructionally Effective Schools." A report of a project sponsored by the School Finance Project of the National Institute of Education, October 1982. In *The Role of the Principal,* pp. 151-182. Hot Topics Series, No. 1. Bloomington, Ind.: Phi Delta Kappa, 1984.

Cohen, M. "Recent Advances in Our Understanding of Schools Effects Research." Paper presented at annual meeting of American Association of College Teacher Education, Chicago, Ill., March, 1979.

Cohen, M. "Effective Schools Research: Towards Useful Interpretations." Paper presented at the Instructional Leadership Conference of the

American Association of School Administrators, Summer 1981.

Cohen, M. "Effective Schools: What the Research Says." *Today's Education* 70, 2 (1981): 38-41.

Cohen, M. "Effective Schools: Accumulating Research Findings." *American Education* 18, 1 (1982): 13-16.

Coker, H.; Medley, D.M.; and Soar, R.S. "How Valid Are Expert Opinions about Effective Teaching?" *Phi Delta Kappan* 62, 2 (1980): 131-134, 149.

Cole, R.W., Jr., ed. "The Editor's Page: Stuck Between the Is and the Ought." *Phi Delta Kappan* 64, 7 (1983): 450.

Cole, R.W., Jr., ed. "The Editor's Page: Filling the Chairs." *Phi Delta Kappan* 64, 10 (1983): 658.

Cole, R.W., Jr., ed. "The Editor's Page: Creating 'Informed Interest' in Education." *Phi Delta Kappan* 65, 3 (1983): 162.

Conger, G.A. "What's a Good Teacher?" *Community and Junior College Journal* 54 (1983-84): 22-25.

Cross, P. "New Roles for College Teachers." *Community College Frontiers* (Winter 1977): 8-12.

Crowson, R.L., and Porter-Gehrie, C. "The Discretionary Behavior of Principals in Large-City Schools." *Education Administration Quarterly* 16, 1 (1980): 45-69.

Crowson, R.L., and Porter-Gehrie, C. "The Urban School Principalship: An Organizational Stability Role." *Planning and Changing* 12, 1 (1981): 26-53.

Cuban, L. "Effective Schools: A Friendly but Cautionary Note." *Phi Delta Kappan* 64, 10 (1983): 695-696.

D'Amico, J. "Using Effective Schools Studies to Create Effective Schools: No Recipe Yet." *Educational Leadership* 40 (1982): 61-62.

De Bevoise, W. "Synthesis of Research on the Principal as Instructional Leader." *Educational Leadership* 41, 5 (1984): 14-20.

Dodd, A.W. "A New Design for Public Education." *Phi Delta Kappan* 65, 10 (1984): 685-687.

Doyle, W. "Classroom Tasks and Students' Abilities." In *Research on Teaching: Concepts, Findings, and Implications,* pp. 183-205. Edited by P. Peterson and H.J. Walberg. Berkeley, Calif.: McCutchan, 1979.

Dunkin, M.J., and Biddle, B.J. *The Study of Teaching.* Washington, D.C.: Holt, Rinehart and Winston, Inc., 1974.

Easton, J.Q.; Barshis, D.; and Ginsberg, R. "Chicago Colleges Identify Effective Teachers, Students." *Community and Junior College Journal* 54, 4 (1983-84): 26-27, 30-31.

Eble, K. *The Aims of College Teaching.* San Francisco: Jossey-Bass, 1983.

Edmonds, R. *A Discussion of the Literature and Issues Related to Effective Schooling.* Paper prepared for National Conference on Urban Education. St. Louis, Mo.: CEMREL Inc., 1978.

Edmonds, R. "Effective Schools for the Urban Poor." *Educational Leadership* 37, 1 (1979): 15-24.

Education Commission of the States. *Action for Excellence.* Washington, D.C.: Author, April 1983.

Elementary School Social Environment and School Achievement. Final Report. East Lansing, Mich.: College of Urban Development, Michigan State University, July 1973.

Elliott, C.D., and Walberg, H.J. "Principal's Competency, Environment and Outcomes." In *Educational Environments and Effects.* Edited by H.J. Walberg. Berkeley, Calif.: McCutchan, 1979.

"Enthusiasm." *Practical Applications of Research* 3, 4 (June 1981): 1-4.

Eubanks, E.E., and Levine, D.U. "A First Look at Effective Schools Projects in New York City and Milwaukee." *Phi Delta Kappan* 64, 10 (1983): 697-702.

Evans, H.D. "We Must Begin Educational Reform 'Every Place at Once.' " *Phi Delta Kappan* 65, 3 (1983): 173-177.

Far West Laboratory. *Educators Probe Issues of Effective Secondary Schools* (Educational R&D Report). San Francisco, Calif.: Author, 1983.

Farrar, E.; Neufeld, B.; and Miles, M.B. "Effective School Programs in High Schools: Social Promotion or Movement by Merit?" *Phi Delta Kappan* 65, 10 (1984): 701-706.

Feinberg, L. "SAT National Average Score Holding Steady After Increase." *Austin American Statesman,* p. A8, September 18, 1983.

Feinberg, L. " 'A Rising Tide of Mediocrity' in U.S." *International Herald Tribune,* pp. 7, 8, 13; May 16, 1984.

Feistritzer, C.E. *The Condition of Teaching: A State-by-State Analysis.* (A Carnegie Foundation Technical Report for the Carnegie Foundation for the Advancement of Teaching). New Jersey: Princeton University Press, 1983.

Fetters, W.B.; Collins, E.F.; and Smith, J.W. *Characteristics Differentiating Under- and Overachieving Elementary Schools.* Technical Note No. 63. Washington, D.C.: Division of Data Analysis and Dissemination, National Center for Educational Statistics, March 12, 1968.

Fincher, C. "What is Learning?" *Engineering Education* 68, 5 (1978): 420-423.

Finn, C.E., Jr. "A Call for Quality Education." *American Education* 18, 1 (1982): 31-36.

Firestone, W.A., and Herriott, R.E. "Prescriptions for Effective Elementary Schools Don't Fit Secondary Schools." *Educational Leadership*

40, 1 (1982): 51-53.

Fiske, E.B. " 'Rising Tide' of School Reports Met by Changes at State Level." *Austin American Statesman,* p. A8, September 18, 1983.

Fonstad, C. *What Research Says About Schools and School Districts... Factors Related to Effectiveness.* Madison, Wis.: Division for Field Services, Wisconsin Department of Public Instruction, October 1973.

Ford Foundation. *City High Schools: A Recognition of Progress.* New York: Author, 1984.

Futrell, M.H. "Towards Excellence." *National Forum* 44 (Spring 1984): 11-24.

Gage, N.L. *The Scientific Basis of the Art of Teaching.* New York: Teachers College Press, Columbia University, 1978.

Gage, N.L. "The Yield of Research on Teaching." *Phi Delta Kappan* 60, 3 (1978): 229-235.

Georgiades, W. *How Good is Your School?* Reston, Va.: National Association of Secondary School Principals, 1978.

Georgiades, W.; Fuentes, E.; and Snyder, K. "A Meta Analysis of Productive School Cultures." Unpublished paper, University of Houston, 1983.

Gersten, R.; Carnine, D.; and Green, S. "The Principal as Instructional Leader: A Second Look." *Educational Leadership* 40, 3 (1982): 47-50.

Gigliotti, R.J., and Brookover, W.B. "The Learning Environment: A Comparison of High and Low Achieving Elementary Schools." *Urban Education* 10 (October 1975): 245-261.

Glassman, E. "The Teacher as Leader." In *New Directions for Teaching and Learning: Improving Teaching Styles* (Number 1), pp. 31-40. Edited by K.E. Eble. San Francisco: Jossey-Bass, Inc., 1980.

"Good Teachers: Sugar and Spice." *Education USA,* December 21, 1981, p. 133.

Good, T.L. "Teacher Expectations and Student Perceptions: A Decade of Research." *Educational Leadership* 38, 5 (1981): 415-422.

Good, T.L. "How Teachers' Expectations Affect Results." *American Education* 18, 10 (1982): 25-32.

Good, T.L.; Biddle, B.J.; and Brophy, J.E. *Teachers Make a Difference.* New York: Holt, Rinehart, and Winston, 1975.

Goodlad, J.I. *A Place Called School: Proposals for the Future.* (A study of schooling in the United States). New York: McGraw-Hill, 1984.

Goodlad, J.I. "A Study of Schooling: Some Findings and Hypotheses." *Phi Delta Kappan* 64, 7 (1983): 465-470.

Goodlad, J.I. "A Study of Schooling: Some Implications for School Improvement." *Phi Delta Kappan* 64, 8 (1983): 521-558.

Gorton, R.A., and McIntyre, K.E. *The Senior High School Principalship, Volume II: The Effective Principal.* Reston, Va.: National Association of Secondary School Principals, 1978.

Greenblatt, R.B.; Cooper, B.S.; and Muth, R. "Managing for Effective Teaching." *Educational Leadership* 41 (1984): 57-59.

Gurney, D.W. "Judging Effective Teaching." *Phi Delta Kappan* 58 (1977): 774-775.

Guskey, T.R., and Easton, J.Q. "The Characteristics of Very Effective Teachers in Urban Community Colleges." *Community/Junior College Quarterly of Research and Practice* 7 (April-June 1983): 265-274.

Hager, J.L., and Scarr, L.E. "Effective Schools—Effective Principals: How to Develop Both." *Educational Leadership* 40, 5 (1983): 38-40.

Hall, G.; Hord, S.M.; Huling, L.L.; Rutherford, W.L.; and Stiegelbauer, S.M. *Leadership Variables Associated with Successful School Improvement* (Tech. Rep. No. 3164). Austin: University of Texas, Research and Development Center for Teacher Education, 1983.

Hall, G.; Hord, S.M.; Guzman, F.M.; Huling Austin, L.; Rutherford, W.L.; and Stiegelbauer, S.M. *The Improvement Process in High Schools: Form, Function, and a Few Surprises* (Tech. Rep. No. 3188). Austin: University of Texas, Research and Development Center for Teacher Education, 1984.

Hall, G.; Rutherford, W.L.; Hord, S.M.; and Huling, L.L. "Effects of Three Principal Styles on School Improvement." *Educational Leadership* 41, 5 (1984): 22-29.

Hoover, M.R. "Characteristics of Black Schools at Grade Level: A Description." *Reading Teacher* (April 1978): 757.

Howe, H., II. "Education Moves to Center Stage: An Overview of Recent Studies." *Phi Delta Kappan* 65, 3 (1983): 167-172.

Hunter, C.S., and Harman, J. *Adult Illiteracy in the United States: A Report to the Ford Foundation.* New York: McGraw-Hill, 1979.

Hurst, D.K. "Of Boxes, Bubbles, and Effective Management." *Harvard Business Review* 62, 3 (1984): 78-88.

Husen, T. "Are Standards in U.S. Schools Really Lagging Behind Those in Other Countries?" *Phi Delta Kappan* 64, 7 (1983): 455-461.

Kash, M.M., and Borich, G.D. *Teacher Behavior and Pupil Self-Concept.* Reading, Mass.: Addison-Wesley Publishing Co., 1978.

Klausmeier, H.J. "A Research Strategy for Educational Improvement." *Educational Researcher* 11, 2 (1982): 8-13.

Klemp, G.O., Jr. "Three Factors of Success." In *Current Issues in Higher Education,* pp. 102-109. Edited by D.W. Vermilye. San Francisco: Jossey-Bass Publishers, 1977.

Klemp, G.O., Jr. "Identifying, Measuring, and Integrating Competence." *New Directions for Experiential Learning* 3 (1979): 41-109.

Klemp, G.O., Jr.; Munger, M.T.; and Spencer, L.M., Jr. *Analysis of Leadership and Management Competencies of Commissioned and Noncommissioned Naval Officers in the Pacific and Atlantic Fleets* (Contract No. N00600-D-0038). Boston, Mass.: McBer & Company, 1977.

Knowles, M. *Self-Directed Learning: A Guide for Learners and Teachers.* Chicago: Follett Publishing Company, 1975.

Kounin, J. *Discipline and Group Management in Classrooms.* New York: Holt, Rinehart, and Winston, 1970.

Kulik, J.A., and Kulik, C.C. "College Teaching." In *Research on Teaching: Concepts, Findings, and Implications,* pp. 70-91. Edited by P. Peterson and H.J. Walberg. Berkeley, Calif.: McCutchan, 1979.

Lapointe, A.E. "The Good News about American Education." *Phi Delta Kappan* 65, 10 (1984): 663-668.

Leithwood, K.A., and Montgomery, D.J. "The Role of the Elementary School Principal in Program Improvement." *Review of Educational Research* 52, 3 (1982): 309-339.

Leonard, G. "The Great 'School Reform' Hoax." *The Charlotte Observer,* pp. 1B, 4B; May 27, 1984.

Levine, D.V.; Levine, R.F.; and Eubanks, E.E. "Characteristics of Effective Inner-City Intermediate Schools." *Phi Delta Kappan* 65, 10 (1984): 707-711.

Lidder, L.H. *Sellitz, Wrightsman & Cook's Research Methods in Social Relations* 4th ed. New York: Holt, Rinehart and Winston, 1981.

Lieberman, A., and Miller, L. "Synthesis of Research on Improving Schools." *Educational Leadership* 38, 7 (1981): 583-586.

Lightfoot, S.L. *The Good High School: Portraits of Character and Culture.* New York: Basic Books, 1983.

Lipham, J.A. *Effective Principal, Effective School.* Reston, Va.: National Association of Secondary School Principals, 1981.

Little, J.W. "The Effective Principal." *American Education* 18 (Aug.-Sept. 1982): 38-42.

Lofland, J. *Analyzing Social Settings.* Belmont, Calif.: Wadsworth Publishing, 1971.

Mackenzie, D.E. "Research for School Improvement: An Appraisal of Some Recent Trends." *Educational Researcher* 12, 4 (April 1983): 5-17.

Manasse, A.L. "Effective Principals. Effective at What?" *Principal* 30, 10 (1982): 14-16.

Manasse, A.L. "Principals as Leaders of High-Performing Systems." *Educational Leadership* 41, 5 (1984): 42-46.

Martin, W.J., and Willower, D.J. "The Managerial Behavior of High School Principals." *Educational Administration Quarterly* 17, 1 (1981): 69-90.

Martin, W.R. "Teacher Behaviors—Do They Make a Difference? A Review of the Research." *Kappa Delta Pi Record* 16 (1979): 48-50, 63.

McClelland, D.C. "Testing for Competence Rather Than for 'Intelligence.' " *American Psychologist* 28, 1 (1973): 1-154.

McCormick, W.J. "Teachers Can Learn to Teach More Effectively." *Educational Leadership* 37, 1 (1979): 59-60.

McCormack-Larkin, M., and Kritch, W.J. "Milwaukee's Project RISE." *Educational Leadership* 40, 3 (1982): 16-21.

McKeachie, W.J., and Kulik, J.A. "Effective College Teaching." In *Review of Research in Education* vol. 3, pp. 165-209. Edited by F.N. Kerlinger. Itasca, Ill.: F.E. Peacock Publishers, Inc., and ASCD, 1975.

Medley, D. "The Effectiveness of Teachers." In *Research on Teaching: Concepts, Findings, and Implications,* pp. 11-27. Edited by P. Peterson and H.J. Walberg. Berkeley, Calif.: McCutchan, 1979.

Miskel, C.G. "Principals' Perceived Effectiveness and Innovation Effort, and the School Situation." *Educational Administration Quarterly* 13, 1 (1977): 31-46.

Miskel, C.G. "Principals' Attitudes toward Work and Coworkers, Situational Factors, Perceived Effectiveness, and Innovation Effort." *Educational Administration Quarterly* 13, 2 (1977): 51-70.

Morgan, E.P. "Effective Teaching in the Urban High School." *Urban Education* 14, 2 (July 1979): 161-181.

Morris, V.; Crowson, R.L.; Hurwitz, E., Jr.; and Porter-Gehrie, C. "The Urban Principal: Middle Manager in the Educational Bureaucracy." *Phi Delta Kappan* 63, 10 (1982): 689-692.

Mosley, M.H., and Smith, P.J. "What Works in Learning? Students Provide the Answers." *Phi Delta Kappan* 63, 4 (1982): 273.

Murphy, J.F.; Weil, M; Hallinger, P.; and Mitman, A. "Academic Press: Translating High Expectations into School Policies and Classroom Practices." *Educational Leadership* 40, 3 (1980): 22-26.

Naisbitt, J. *Megatrends: Ten New Directions Transforming Our Lives.* New York: Warner Books, 1982.

National Commission on Excellence in Education. *A Nation at Risk: The Imperative for Education Reform.* Washington, D.C.: USPGO, 1983.

New York City Board of Education. *School Improvement Project: The Case Study Phase.* New York: School Improvement Project, 1979.

New York Office of Education Performance Review. *School Factors Influencing Reading Achievement: A Case Study of Two Inner City Schools.* Albany, N.Y.: Author, March 1974.

"Newsnotes." *Phi Delta Kappan* 65, 3 (1983): 229-230.

Nystrand, R.O. "Leadership Theories for Principals." *Theory Into Practice* 20, 4 (1981): 260-263.

Odden, A. "Research Findings on Effective Teaching and Schools." *Issuegram*, Series 303-830-3842, Report 1, 1983.

Office of Program Evaluation and Research. *California School Effectiveness, Study, the First Year.* Sacramento, Calif.: California State Department of Education, 1977.

Office of Program Evaluation and Research. *Report on the Special Studies of Selected ECE Schools with Increasing and Decreasing Reading Scores.* Sacramento, Calif.: California State Department of Education, 1980.

Oppel, R.A., et al., eds. "Literacy Barrier: CPCC Seeks a Breakthrough." *The Charlotte Observer*, July 18, 1983.

Ornstein, A.C. "How Good Are Teachers in Affecting Student Outcomes? Part I." *NASSP Bulletin* 58 (1982): 61-70.

Ornstein, A.C. "How Good Are Teachers in Affecting Student Outcomes? Part II." *NASSP Bulletin* 59 (1983): 73-80.

Ornstein, A.C., and Levine, D.V. "Teacher Behavior Research. Overview and Outlook." *Phi Delta Kappan* 62 (1981): 592-596.

Ornstein, A.C., and Miller, H.L. *Looking into Teaching.* Chicago: Rand McNally College Publishing Co., 1980.

Passow, A.H. "Tackling the Reform Problems of the 1980s." *Phi Delta Kappan* 65, 10 (1984): 674-683.

Perot, H.R. "Changing Texas Education System to Be Difficult." *The Dallas Morning News*, September 11, 1983.

Persell, C.H., and Cookson, P.W., Jr. "The Effective Principal in Action." In *The Effective Principal: A Research Summary.* Reston, Va.: National Association of Secondary School Principals, 1982.

Peters, T.J., and Waterman, R.H., Jr. *In Search of Excellence.* New York: Harper and Row, 1982.

Peters, T.J., and Waterman, R.H., Jr. "A Bias for Action." *Best of Business* 5, 1 (1983): 6-12.

Peterson, P. "Direct Instruction Reconsidered." In *Research on Teaching: Concepts, Findings, and Implications*, pp. 57-69. Edited by P. Peterson and H.J. Walberg. Berkeley, Calif.: McCutchan, 1979.

Phi Delta Kappa. *Why Do Some Urban Schools Succeed?* The Phi Delta Kappa Study of Exceptional Urban Elementary Schools. Birmingham, Ind.: Author, 1980.

Pinero, U.C. "Wanted: Strong Instructional Leaders." *Principal* 61, 4 (1982): 16-19.

Pipho, C. "Stateline: A Year of Transition for Education." *Phi Delta Kappan* 65, 10 (1984): 661-662.

Pratzner, F.C. "Quality of School Life: Foundations for Improvement." *Educational Researcher* 13, 3 (1984): 20-25.

Purkey, S.C., and Smith, M.S. "Too Soon to Cheer? Synthesis of Research on Effective Schools." *Educational Leadership* 40, 3 (1982): 64-69.

Ralph, J.H., and Fennessey, J. "Science or Reform: Some Questions About the Effective Schools Model." *Phi Delta Kappan* 64, 10 (1983): 689-694.

Ravitch, Diane. *The Troubled Crusade: American Education, 1945-1980.* New York: Basic Books, 1983.

Raywid, M.A. "Schools of Choice: Their Current Nature and Prospects." *Phi Delta Kappan* 64, 10 (1983): 684-746.

"Report on Excellence in Education Acclaimed: Panelists Criticize Reagan's Interpretation." *Chronicle of Higher Education,* May 11, 1983, pp. 1, 10.

Research Action Brief, Number 23. ERIC Clearinghouse on Educational Management. (ERIC Document Reproduction Service No. EA 016 193), February 1984.

Resnick, D.P., and Resnick, L.B. "Improving Educational Standards in American Schools." *Phi Delta Kappan* 65, 3 (1983): 178-180.

Rogers, V.; Talbot, C.; and Cosgrove, E. "Excellence: Some Lessons from America's Best Run Companies." *Educational Leadership* 41, 5 (1984): 39-41.

Rosenshine, B.V. "Content, Time and Direct Instruction." In *Research on Teaching: Concepts, Findings, and Implications,* pp. 28-56. Edited by P. Peterson and H.J. Walberg. Berkeley, Calif.: McCutchan, 1979.

Rosenshine, B., and Furst, N. "Research on Teacher Performance Criteria." In *Research in Teacher Education: A Symposium,* p. 890. Edited by B. Othanel Smith. New York: Prentice-Hall, Inc., 1971.

Rotberg, I.C. "A New Perspective on Math and Science Education." *Phi Delta Kappan* 65, 10 (1984): 669-669.

Roueche, J.E. "The Need for Excellence in College Teaching." In *Promoting Great Teaching: A Staff Development Imperative, Proceedings of the Institute on Staff Development,* pp. 18-23, 1982.

Roueche, J.E. "Toward Achieving Excellence." *Innovation Abstracts* V, 29 (October 14, 1983).

Roueche, J.E.; Baker, G.A.; and Roueche, S.D. *College Responses to Low-Achieving Students: A National Study.* Orlando, Fl.: HBJ Media Systems Corporation, 1984.

Rowan, B.; Bossert, S.T.; and Dwyer, D.C. "Research on Effective Schools: A Cautionary Note." *Educational Researcher* 12, 4 (1983): 24-31.

Rubel, Robert J., ed. *HEW's Safe School Study.* College Park, Md.: Institute of Reduction of Crime, 1978.

Rutherford, W.L.; Hord, S.M.; Huling, L.L.; and Hall, G. *Change Facilitators: In Search of Understanding Their Role* (Tech. Rep. No. 3159). Austin: University of Texas, Research and Development Center for Teacher Education, 1983.

Rutter, M.; Maughan, P.M.; and Ouston, J. *Fifteen Thousand Hours.* Cambridge, Mass.: Harvard University Press, 1979.

Sanford, J.P.; Emmer, E.T.; and Clements, B.S. "Improving Classroom Management." *Educational Leadership* 40, 7 (1983): 56-60.

Sarason, S.B. *Schooling in America: Scapegoat and Salvation.* New York: Free Press, 1983.

Schneider, J.E. *Researchers Discover Formula for Success in Student Learning (Educational R&D Report).* San Francisco, Calif.: Far West Laboratory, 1979.

Schneider, C.; Klemp, G.O.; and Kastendiek, S. *The Balancing Act: Competencies of Effective Teachers and Mentors in Degree Programs for Adults.* Chicago: Center for Continuing Education; Boston: McBer and Company, 1981.

Schneider, C.; Klemp, G.O.; and Kastendiek, S. "The Balancing Act: Competencies of Effective Teachers and Mentors." *Innovation Abstracts* V, 4 (February 1984).

Schools Can Make a Difference. East Lansing, Mich.: College of Urban Renewal, Michigan State University, 1977.

Scully, M.G. "Raising College Standard Is Already in the Works." *Chronicle of Higher Education,* 10 (May 11, 1983): 1.

Selection Research, Inc. *Teacher Perceiver Interview Manual.* Lincoln, Neb.: Author, 1979.

Sergiovanni, T.J. "Leadership and Excellence in Schooling." *Educational Leadership* 41, 5 (1984): 6-13.

Shoemaker, J.; and Fraser, H.W. "What Principals Can Do: Some Implications from Studies of Effective Schooling." *Phi Delta Kappan,* 63, 3 (1981): 178-182.

Silberman, C.E. *Crisis in the Classroom.* New York: Random House, 1970.

Sizer, T.R. "High School Reform: The Need for Engineering." *Phi Delta Kappan* 64, 10 (1983): 679-683.

Sizer, T.R. *Horace's Compromise: The Dilemma of the American High School Today.* Boston: Houghton Mifflin, 1984.

Smith, V.H. "Books: This Close-Up Look at Schooling Yields Radical Proposals for Change." *Phi Delta Kappan* 64, 3 (1983): 226-228.

Snyder, K.J. "Instructional Leadership for Productive Schools." *Educational Leadership* 40, 5 (1983): 32-37.

Snyder, K.J. "Preparing Principals to Manage Productive Schools: A Neglected Dimension of Teacher Education." *Journal of Teacher Education* 35, 2 (1984): 55-57.

Soar, R.S., and Soar, R.M. "Emotional Climate and Management." In *Research on Teaching: Concepts, Findings, and Implications,* pp. 97-119. Edited by P. Peterson and H.J. Walberg. Berkeley, Calif.: McCutchan 1979.

Solorzano, L. "What's Wrong with Our Teachers." *U.S. News & World Report,* March 1983, pp. 37-40.

Spencer, L.M. *The Navy Leadership and Management Education and Training Program.* Unpublished manuscript, 1977.

Squires, D.A.; Huitt, W.G.; and Segars. *Effective Schools and Classrooms: A Research-Based Perspective.* Alexandria, Va.: Association for Supervision and Curriculum Development, 1979.

Stallings, J. "Allocated Academic Learning Time Revisited, or Beyond Time on Task." *Educational Researcher* 9 (December 1980): 11-16.

Stallings, J. *What Research Has to Say to Administrators of Secondary Schools About Effective Teaching and Staff Development, p. 8. (ERIC Document Reproduction No. ED 209 748),* July 1981.

Stow, S. "Using Effectiveness Research in Teacher Evaluation." *Educational Leadership* 37, 1 (1979): 55-56, 58.

Strother, D.B. "The Many Roles of the Effective Principal." *Phi Delta Kappan* 65, 4 (1983): 291-294.

Strother, D.B. "Homework: Too Much, Just Right, or Not Enough?" *Phi Delta Kappan* 65, 10 (1984): 423-426.

Strother, D.B. "Practical Applications of Research: Another Look at Time-on-Task." *Phi Delta Kappan* 65, 10 (1984): 714-717.

Sweeney, J. "Principals Can Provide Instructional Leadership—It Takes Commitment." *Education* 103, 2 (1982): 204-207.

Sweeney, J. "Research Synthesis on Effective School Leadership." *Educational Leadership* 39, 5 (1982): 346-352.

Task Force on Education for Economic Growth. *Action for Excellence.* Washington, D.C.: Education Commission of the States, 1983.

Tishler, A.G., and Palmer, R.W. "Effective Teaching: Kadelpians vs. Principals" *Kappa Delta Pi Record* 20 (Summer 1984): 109-112.

Toch, T. "For School Reforms Top Salesman, It's Been Some Year." *Education Week,* June 6, 1984, pp. 1, 33.

Tomlinson, T.M. "Effective Schools: Mirror or Mirage." *Today's Education* 70, 2 (1981): 38-41.

Tomlinson, T.M. "Review of Creating Effective Schools." *Educational Leadership* 40 (1982): 72-73.

Troisi, N.F. *Effective Teaching and Student Achievement.* Reston, Va.: National Association of Secondary School Principals. (ERIC Document Reproduction Service No. ED 231 067), 1979.

Tye, K.A., and Tye, B.B. "Teacher Isolation and School Reform" *Phi Delta Kappan* 65, 5 (1984): 319-322.

Tyler, R.W. "A Place Called School." *Phi Delta Kappan* 64, 7 (1983): 462-470.

United States Department of Education. *The Nation Responds: Recent Efforts to Improve Education.* Washington, D.C.: Author, 1984.

Vallina, S.A. *Analysis of Observed Critical Task Performance of Title I-ESEA Principals, State of Illinois.* Unpublished Ed.D. dissertation, University of Florida, 1970.

Venezky, R.L., and Winfield, L.F. *Schools That Succeed Beyond Expectations in Teaching Reading.* University of Delaware Studies on Education, Technical Report No. 1. Newark, Del.: Department of Educational Studies, University of Delaware, August 1979.

Walberg, H.J., and Fredrick, W.C. "Instructional Time and Learning." In *Encyclopedia of Educational Research* 5th ed., vol. 2, pp. 917-924. Edited by H.E. Mitzel. New York: The Free Press, 1982.

Ware, B.A. "What Rewards Do Students Want?" *Phi Delta Kappan* 59, 5 (January 1978): 355-356.

Weber, G. *Inner-City Children Can Be Taught to Read: Four Successful Schools.* Occasional Papers Number Eighteen, Washington, D.C.: Council for Basic Education, October 1971.

Weick, K. "Educational Organizations as Loosely Coupled Systems.' *Administrative Science Quarterly* 21, 1 (1976): 1-19.

Weick, K. "Administering Education in Loosely Coupled Schools.' *Phi Delta Kappan* 63, 10 (1982): 673-676.

Wellborn, S.N. "Ahead: A Nation of Illiterates?" *U.S. News & World Report,* May 1982, pp. 53-57.

West, E., ed. "The Highwire 100." *Highwire,* Spring 1983, pp. 22-28.

Westbrook, J.D. *Considering the Research: What Makes an Effective School?* Paper written for NIE, contract No. 400-80-0107 (Project A-1). Austin, Tex.: Southwest Educational Development Laboratory, September 1982.

White, H.D., and Calhoun, K. "Mapping a Curriculum by Computer." *Journal of the American Society for Information Science* 35, 2 (1984): 82-89.

Wicker, T. "Colleges Ask Students for Less." *Salisbury Post,* March 26, 1983.

Williams, D.A., et al., "Can the Schools Be Saved?" *Newsweek,* May 1983, pp. 50-58.

Winn, I. "High School Reform: Stuffing the Turkeys." *Phi Delta Kappan* 65, 3 (1983): 184-185.

Wynne, E.A. "Looking at Good Schools" *Phi Delta Kappan* 62 (January 1981): 377-381.

Yukl, G. "Managerial Leadership and the Effective Principal." In *The Effective Principal: A Research Summary*, pp. 1-13. Reston, Va.: National Association of Secondary School Principals, 1982.

Zigli, B. "High School's 'Weak Link' in Chain." *USA Today*, May 13, 1983, pp. 1A, 2A.

ACKNOWLEDGMENTS

I t would be impossible to cite all of the individuals who contributed to this work, but several deserve special recognition and thanks.

Patricia Mullin and Nancy Hess Omaha Boy have served admirably as senior researchers with us on the Richardson study. Each brought to the project many years of teaching experience in both American public schools and community colleges. They have made major contributions to the study through their data collection and analysis efforts and by their contributions to the final manuscript.

Valleau Wilkie Jr. of the Sid Richardson Foundation believed in the project's worth from the beginning of our discussions with him. Indeed, it was his suggestion that "we take a look at the state of teaching in American public schools." Without his support and critical input, this study would never have been undertaken.

Special thanks go to the Honorable T. H. Bell, Past Secretary of Education and to his SSRP staff (especially Pat McKee) in the Department of Education for initial interest in and support of the study.

We gratefully acknowledge Jacquelyn A. McGee, principal of Austin High School, Texas, who helped us greatly during the formative stages of our study with a variety of strategies for evaluating teachers. She also made available to us the Austin Independent School District Faculty Evaluation Procedure. For assistance in summarizing the various education reform reports, thanks go to Dean John Weber of Central Oregon Community College, who spent part of his sabbatical at The University of Texas at Austin as a reviewer on this project. Similar recognition goes to Ann Parish, herself a model of teaching excellence at Johnston High School, Austin, Texas, for her reviews and summaries of research on leadership and teaching, and to Michael Burke, an administrator at Eastfield College, Dallas, Texas, who found time away from his dissertation pursuits to review for us studies of organizational climate and culture. Jackie Lovette provided us statistical advice and data interpretation.

A number of our University of Texas at Austin faculty and staff colleagues provided assistance and input throughout the study. Elizabeth Savage assisted with selection of computer hardware and software and provided expert word processing. She and Libby Lord also diligently documented, proofed, and produced our first manuscript. Nanci Bernbrock provided thoughtful editing and fastidious attention to the infinite details involved in producing our final manuscript. Ruth Thompson aided with the installation of computer hardware helping us to work out all the "bugs" in the system. Thanks also to Reid Watson for his assistance throughout the project.

To Suanne D. Roueche and Lynn B. Burnham, both with The National Institute for Staff and Organizational Development (NISOD) at The University of Texas at Austin, go our most special thanks and recognition for the countless editions of chapters and manuscripts they read, edited, and re-read. Their suggestions added greatly to the quality of our final manuscript.

We could never properly acknowledge the devotion, dedication, and commitment of the principals and teachers in the secondary schools who volunteered to participate in our study. Each of them spent countless hours sharing with us successful efforts to improve teaching quality in their schools and classrooms. We felt from the beginning that only "the best of the best" would take the time and make the effort. They indeed epitomize excellence in American schools. All of these participants are listed in Appendices B and C. Without the support and assistance of these friends and colleagues, this work could not have been completed.

AASA would like to acknowledge the efforts of the staff members who contributed to the publication of this book. AASA Executive Director, Richard D. Miller; Associate Executive Directors Joseph J. Scherer and Jerry Melton reviewed the initial manuscript. Senior Executive Administrator for Federal Initiatives, Herman R. Goldberg, reviewed the initial and final manuscripts and made frequent suggestions. AASA Associate Executive Director, and Director of Communications, Gary Marx, served as project director. AASA Publications Manager, Anne Dees, served as primary editor. Cindy Tursman, editor of *The School Administrator*, and AASA Managing Editor, Joanne Kaldy, also reviewed the manuscript. Communications Unit Coordinator, Karen Ellzey, worked with the printers.

ABOUT THE
AUTHORS

JOHN E. ROUECHE is professor of educational administration and Director of the Community College Leadership Program at The Unversity of Texas at Austin. He is the author of more than 100 books, monographs, and articles focused on educational leadership and teaching effectiveness. Two of his books, *Overcoming Learning Problems*, 1977, and *College Responses to Low-Achieving Students*, 1984 (with George A. Baker III and Suanne D. Roueche) earned him the Council of Universities and Colleges Outstanding Research Publication Awards. He also received the 1984 Distinguished Research Award from the National Association of Developmental Education and the 1985 University of Texas Outstanding Researcher Award. He received The University of Texas at Austin Teaching Excellence Award in 1982.

In great demand as a conference and convention keynote speaker, Roueche has spoken to more than 1,100 college, university, and public school faculties since 1970.

As Project Director of the National Institute for Staff and Organizational Development, Roueche has spearheaded the establishment of a national network of more than 400 colleges and universities committed to the improvement of teaching effectiveness and to the professional growth and development of teachers and administrators. In 1980 a national study at Florida State University identified him as the outstanding living author in the field of community college education.

GEORGE A. BAKER III is associate professor of educational administration at The University of Texas at Austin, where he was selected as the 1983 recipient of The University's Teaching Excellence Award. A former member of the White House staff under President Lyndon Johnson, Baker taught on the faculties of the U.S. Naval War College, The University of Virginia, and Furman University. He has also served as Vice President for Academic Affairs at Greenville Technical College (S.C.) and as the founding director of the National Institute for Staff and Organizational Development (NISOD), at The University of Texas at Austin.

A prolific researcher, writer, and public speaker, Baker was honored in 1984 by the Council of Universities and Colleges for the results of his national study (with Roueche and Roueche) of college programs for underprepared students. In 1984, he was also selected to teach the first undergraduate honors course in the College of Education at The University of Texas at Austin.

PATRICIA L. MEYER MULLIN is currently associate dean at Fort Steilacoom Community College, Tacoma, Washington. She has extensive teaching experience in both high school and junior high school followed by faculty experience at The University of Iowa. She served on the faculty of Lane Community College (Oregon) for a number of years and later taught at The University of Oregon in Eugene. Prior to her work at The University of Texas at Austin, she taught in high schools in Alexandria, Egypt, and then later at the Saudi Arabian International School in Dhahran, Saudi Arabia. She completed her Ph.D. in educational administration in August 1985.

NANCY HESS OMAHA BOY is dean at Wenatchee Valley College, Omak, Washington. She joined the research staff at The University after having served as Provost of the McConnell Air Force Base Campus with Butler County Community College (Kansas). She also served as Professor and Acting Chair in the Department of Education at Sinte Gleska College, South Dakota, and earlier directed educational programs for the Wisconsin Winnebago Tribe. She has teaching experience abroad and has extensive background in the development of programs and courses for native American populations in Wisconsin and South Dakota.